America's Restless Ghosts

America's
Restless
Ghosts

---

*Photographic Evidence for
Life After Death*

Hans Holzer

Longmeadow Press

Published by Longmeadow Press, 201 High Ridge Road, Stamford, CT 06904

Cover design by Allan Mogel

Interior design by Allan Mogel

Library of Congress Cataloging- in- Publication Data

Holzer, Hans

   America's restless ghosts / by Hans Holzer.-- 1st ed.

     p. cm.

   ISBN 0-681-45231-5

   1. Spirit photography -- United States. 2. Ghosts--United States.

 I. Title.

 Bf1381.h563 1993

 133.9'2--dc20

Printed in United States of America

0 9 8 7 6 5 4 3 2 1

TABLE OF CONTENTS

PART TWO

America's Restless Ghosts

INTRODUCTION

Except for committed magicians and total materialists, most reasonable people consider the possibility of life continuing beyond death an important question.

Equally, most people, except uncritical "believers," will not really care that much about any serious scientifically oriented approach to the question of life eternal, or at least, an existence beyond the dissolution of the body as we commonly understand it.

I, of course, am in the middle: I do require reasonable proof, convincing evidence for the existence of another dimension into which all of us must pass, and, moreover, the nature of that further dimension, and the terms of our entering it.

Nothing can be more convincing than authentic, genuine evidence of that world "next door," as described by Eileen Garrett, than photographs—provided they are taken under conditions excluding any and all possibility of concious fraud, unconscious delusion, error, so-called coincidence and any explanation of them *other* than that they are indeed the real pictures of people who have gone from this world into the next.

There is nothing in this work that does not meet those stringent criteria, no matter how odd some of the photographs may seem to the untrained observer.

I have spent 50 years collecting this research—from my days as a student to today—and in the course of this work learned the tricks of the trickster trade. Of course there are fraudulent pictures, too, and pictures that appear to be unusual only in the mind of the beholder who took them. But my standards are firm: judge for yourself. These are the photographs of ghosts, spirits, discarnates—people like you and I, who have passed on to the next stage of existence and have, for a variety of reasons, communicated with this level of consciousness through photographic means.

Prof. Hans Holzer, Ph.D.

Parapsychologist

PART
ONE

I
COMMUNICATIONS FROM BEYOND THROUGH PHOTOGRAPHY: TRACK RECORD AND TEST CONDITIONS

For the past 100 years, psychic research has painstakingly assembled proof for the continuance of life and has gradually emerged from a metaphysical mantle into the full glare of scientific inquiry. Although various researchers interpret the results of these investigations according to their own attitudes toward survival of human personality, it is no longer possible to bury the evidence itself, as some materialistically inclined scientists in other fields have attempted to do over the years. The challenge is always present: does man have a soul, scientifically speaking, and if so, how can we prove it?

Material on communications with the so-called dead is very large and, to me, often convincing, though not necessarily all of it in the way it is sometimes presented by partisans of the spiritualist religion. But additional proof that man does continue an existence in what Dr. Joseph Rhine, then of Duke University, has called "the world of the mind" was always wanted, especially the kind of proof that could be viewed objectively without the need for subjective observation through psychic experiences, either spontaneous or induced in the laboratory. One of the greatest potential tools was given man when photography was invented: for if we could photograph the dead under conditions that carefully exclude trickery, we would surely be so much the wiser — and the argument for survival would indeed be stronger.

Photography itself goes back to the 1840s, when the technique evolved gradually from very crude light-and-shadow pictures, through daguerreotypes and tintypes to photography as we now know it.

Major Tom Patterson, a British psychic researcher, in a booklet entitled *Spirit Photography,* has dealt with the beginnings of photographic mediumship in Britain, where it has produced the largest amount of experimental material in the century since.

But the initial experiment took place in 1862, in Boston, not Britain. 23 years after photography itself came into being. William H. Mumler, an engraver, who was neither interested in nor a believer in spiritualism or any other form of psychic research, had been busy in his off hours experimenting with a camera. At that time the photographic camera was still a novelty. The engraver liked to take snapshots of his family and friends to learn more about his camera. Imagine Mumler's surprise and dismay when some of his negatives showed faces that were not supposed to be on them. In addition to the living people he had so carefully posed and photographed, Mumler discovered the portraits of dead relatives alongside the "normal" portraits.

This was the beginning of psychic photography. It happened accidentally – if there is such a thing as an accident in our well-organized universe – and the news of Mumler's unsought achievements spread across the world. Other photographers, both professionals and amateurs, discovered talents similar to Mumler's, and the psychic research societies in Britain and America began to take notice of this amazing development.

Since then a great many changes have taken place in the technology and we have greater knowledge of its pitfalls. But the basic principle of photography is still the same: film covered with silver salts is exposed to the radiation called light and reacts to it. This reaction results in certain areas of the emulsion being eaten away, leaving an exact replica of the image seen by the camera lens on the photographic film. Depending on the intensity with which light hits the various portions of the film, the eating away of silver salts will vary, thus rendering the tones and shadings of the resulting negative on light-sensitive photographic paper and hence the positive print, which is a mechanical reproduction of the negative's light and shadow areas, but in reverse.

To make a print, the operator merely inserts the finished negative into a printer, places the light-sensitive paper underneath the negative and exposes it through the negative with an electric light. Noth-

14

ing new can be added in this manner, nor can anything already on the negative be taken away, but the skill of the craftsman operating the printer will determine how well balanced the resulting positive print will be, depending on the duration and intensity of the printing lamp.

Most people who are photographers know these simple facts, but there are many who are not, and for whom this information might be useful.

The obtaining of any sort of images on photographic paper, especially recognizable pictures such as faces or figures, without having first made a negative in the usual manner is, of course, a scientific impossibility—*except* in psychic photography.

Until the arrival on the scene of Polaroid cameras and Polaroid film, this was certainly 100 percent true. The Polaroid method, with its instant result and development of film within a matter of a few seconds after exposure, adds the valuable element of close supervision to an experiment. It also allows an even more direct contact between psychic radiation and sensitive surface. The disadvantage of Polaroid photography is its ephemeral character. Even the improved film does not promise to stay unspoiled forever, and it is wise to protect unusual Polaroid photographs by obtaining slide copies. Actually, Polaroid photography uses a combination of both film and sensitive paper simultaneously, one being peeled off the other after the instant development process inside the camera.

Fakery with the ordinary type of photograhy would depend on double exposure or double printing by unscrupulous operators, in which case no authentic negative could be produced that would stand up to *experienced* scrutiny. Fakery with Polaroid equipment is impossible if camera, film and operator are closely watched. Because of the great light sensitivity of Polaroid film, double exposure, if intended, is not a simple matter, as one exposure would severly cancel out the other and certainly leave traces of double exposure. And the film, of course, would have to be switched in the presence of the observer, something not even a trained conjurer is likely to do to an experienced psychic investigator. A psychic researcher must also be familiar with magic and sleight-of-hand tricks, in order to qualify for that title.

The important thing to remember about psychic photography is that the bulk of it occurred unexpectedly and often embarrassingly to amateur photographers not the least bit interested in parapsychology or any form of occultism. The extras on the negatives were not placed there by these people to confuse themselves. They were the portraits of dead relatives or friends that could be recognized. The literature on this phase of psychic photography, notably in Britain, is impressive; and I particularly recommend the scholarly work by F. W. Warrick, the celebrated British parapsychologist, called *Experiments in Psychics*, in which hundreds of experimental photographs are reproduced. Warrick's, work published in 1939 by E. P. Dutton, deals primarily with the photographic mediumship of Emma Deane, although other examples are included. Warrick points out that he and his colleagues, having spent some 30 years working with and closely supervising their subjects, knew their personal habits and quirks. Any kind of trickery was therefore out of the question, unless one wanted to call a researcher who propounded unusual ideas self-deluded or imcompetent, as some latter-day critics have done to Harry Price and Sir William Crookes, respected British psychic researchers now dead.

Any person who is not present when the original experiments or investigations take place and who does not possess firsthand knowledge of the conditions and processes of that investigation is no more qualified to judge its results than an armchair strategist trying to rewrite history. Although Patterson's booklet frankly uses the scientific evidence at hand to support the spiritualistic view, it also serves as a useful source of factual information. Mumler's record as the "first" spirit photographer is upheld by U.S. Court of Appeals Judge John Edmond, who investigated Mumler personally and obtained photographs under test conditions of people known only to him who were dead. Originally, Judge Edmond had gone into the investigation thinking it was all a deception. In a letter published by the *New York Herald* on August 6, 1853, however, the judge spoke not only of Mumler's experiments but also of his subsequent sittings with well-known mediums of his day. These investigations convinced him that spiritualism had a valid base, and he became a confirmed believer from then on, displaying some psychic abilities of his own as time went by.

In England, the craft of psychic photography developed slowly from the 1870s onward. The first person in Britain to show successful results in this field was Frederick Hudson, who in 1872 produced a number of authentic likenesses of the dead under conditions excluding fraud. Several experiments were undertaken under the careful scrutiny of Dr. Alfred Russel Wallace, a famed naturalist in his day. Wallace attested to the genuineness of the observed phenomena. Since then several dozen talented psychic photographers have appeared on the scene, producing for a few pennies genuine likenesses of persons known to have died previously in the presence of "sitters" (or portrait subjects) they had never before met in their lives.

As the craft became better known and men of science wondered about it, researchers devised more and more rigid test conditions for this type of experimental psychic photography. Film, paper, cameras, developing fluid – in short, all implements necessary to produce photographs of any kind – were furnished, controlled and held by uncommitted researchers. The medium was not allowed to touch anything and was kept at a distance from the camera and film. In many cases he was not even present in the room itself. Nevertheless psychic "extras" kept appearing on the properly exposed film and were duly recognized as the portraits of dead persons, often of obscure identity, but traceable as relatives or friends of someone present. Occasionally, as with John Myers, America's leading psychic photographer, in his early days the portraits thus obtained by the photographic medium were strangers to all concerned until the pictures were first published in *Psychic News*, a leading spiritualist newspaper of the day. Only then did the "owners" of the psychic "extras" write in to the editor to claim their dead relatives!

Despite the overwhelming evidence that these photographs were genuine – in almost all cases even the motive for fraud was totally absent – some researchers kept rejecting then – and indeed they do now – the possibility that the results were nothing but fraudulently manufactured double exposures. Even so brilliant a person as Eileen Garrett, president of Parapsychology Foundation, insisted for many years that all psychic photographs *had* to be fraudulent, having been so informed by a pair of self-styled experts. It was only when I myself produced the photographs of ghosts, and acquainted Mrs. Garrett with the camera, film and other details of how the pictures were obtained, that she reluctantly agreed that we had indeed "made a breakthrough" in the field of psychic photography. Prejudice against anything involving a major shift in one's thinking, philosophy of life and general training is much stronger than we dare admit to ourselves sometimes.

Often psychic photography also occurs at so-called home circles where neither money nor notoriety is involved and where certainly no need exists for self-delusion by those taking the pictures. They are, presumably, already convinced of survival of personality after death, otherwise they would not be members of the circle.

Photographs of ghosts or haunted areas are much rarer because of the great element of chance in obtaining any results at all. Whereas psychic photography in the experimental sense is subject to schedules and human plans, the taking of ghost pictures is not. Even I had neither advance knowledge nor control over the ones I managed to obtain, and I could not do it again that way if I tried.

We still don't know *all* of the conditions that make these extraordinary photographs possible and, until we do, obtaining them will be a hit-and-miss affair at best. But the fact that genuine photographs of what are commonly called ghosts have been taken by a number of people, under conditions excluding fraud or faulty equipment, of course, is food for serious thought.

An example in recent years is the photograph of a Danish sailor fighting for his life at Ballyheigue Castle, Ireland, taken by a vacationing army officer named Captain P. D. O'Donnell, on June 4, 1962. Unbeknownst to O'Donnell, that was the anniversary of the sailor's death during the so-called silver raid, in which the silver stored at the castle was stolen by local bandits and fighting ensued. O'Donnell took this snapshot without thought or knowledge of ghosts, while inspecting the ruins of the once proud castle. The picture was later lost in transit and could not be located by the post office.

Many newspapers the world over, including *The People* of July 3, 1966, reported and published a ghost photograph taken by 18-year-old Gordon Carroll in St. Mary the Virgin Church, Woodford, Northhamptonshire, England. The picture clearly shows a monk kneeling before the altar, but at the time he took it Carroll was the only person inside the church. Fortunately, he found an understanding ear in the person of Canon John Pearce-Higgins, Provost of Southwark Cathedral and a member of the Church's Fellowship of Psychical and Physical Research. Pearce-Higgins, after inspecting camera and film and questioning the young man, was satisfied that the phenomenon was authentic. Carroll used a tripod and a brand-new Ilford Sportsman Rangefinder camera. He loaded it with Agfa C.T.18 film, which he often used to photograph stained-glass windows in churches, a hobby of his. The Agfa Company, on examining the film, confirmed that trick photography had not been used and that neither film nor developing showed any faults. As for the ghost, no one seems to have bothered to find out who he was. The church itself is a very ancient place, mentioned in the *Domesday Book*, a list of important properties compiled under William the Conqueror. A church stood on that spot even before the Norman conquest of Britain, so it is quite possible that at one time or other a monk died there, tragically becoming the ghost that Carroll's camera accidentally saw and recorded.

Joe Hyams, writer-husband of actress Elke Sommer, shared a haunted house with her for some time in Hollywood, only to give up to the ghost in the end. During the last stages of their occupancy, phogographer Allan Grant, strictly a nonbeliever, took some pictures in the aftermath of a fire of mysterious origin. The pictures, published in *The Saturday Evening Post* of June 3, 1967, clearly show manifestations not compatible with ordinary photographic results.

The very latest development in the area of psychic photography, although not concerned with images of ghosts, is still germane to the entire question. Thought forms registering on photographic film or other light-sensitive surfaces are the result of years of hard work by Colorado University's Professor Jule Eisenbud, a well-known psychiatrist interested in parapsychology as well, with Chicago photographic medium Ted Serios. These amazing pictures were published in 1989 by Eisenbud in an impressive volume called *The World of Ted Serios.* In addition, more material has become available as the experiments continued, thanks to the efforts of a number of universities and study groups who have belatedly recognized the importance of this type of experiment.

Serios has the ability of projecting images of objects and scenes often at great distances in space, or even *time* onto film or a TV tube. This includes places he has never visited or seen before. Eisenbud does not suggest that there are spirit forces at work here. He merely points out, quite rightly, that we do not as yet realize some of the areas in which the human mind can operate. Without having been present at the many sessions in which Eisenbud and a host of other scientists subjected Serios to every conceivable test, I cannot judge the results. But it appears to me from what I have read in the book, and from other Serios photographs shown to me privately, that Serios is capable of astral projection. In these out-of-the-body states he does visit distant places in a flash, then almost instantly returns to his physical body and records the impressions received by his etheric eyes onto Polaroid film. Above all, I feel that Serios is one of an impressive line of photography mediums.

There may be differences of opinion concerning the implications of psychic photography, with some quarters taking the attitude that it merely represents a record of past events that somehow got left behind in the atmosphere during the event itself. This is undoubtedly possible in a number of cases. But there are also an impressive number of other instances where this view does not fit and where only the unpopular theory (scientifically speaking) of survival of human personality in a thought world will satisfy as an explanation. Either way, psychic photography, like it or not, is the very threshold of a new science.

II
THE MEDIUMSHIP
OF JOHN MYERS

The *possibility* of fraud is always present when planned experiments take place. But the possibility of an explosion is also always present when munitions are being manufactured, and nobody stops making them. One simply proceeds with great care in both cases. Magicians and other conjurers have assaulted psychic photography as patently fake, since *they* could fake it. This, of course, is a neat trick. By suggesting the possibility as the probability, these limited individuals (spiritually speaking) miss the point of scientifically controlled experiments in psychic photography: it is not what *could* be that matters, but what actually *does* happen.

I have no valid reason to doubt the majority of the older psychic photographs I have examined but, since I was not present when they were taken and have no way of knowing how rigid the controls were at the time, I will not personally vouch for them. This does not mean that they are not genuine. It does mean that anything I vouch for has occurred in my presence and/or under my controls and with persons known to me under conditions generally considered appropriate by professional parapsychologists. When I studied the literature on this subject, notably Warrick's work on *Experiments in Psychics,* I was impressed by the sincerity of Warrick's approach and by his sensible controls through which he made sure that his subjects could not obtain their amazing results by trickery of any kind. Warrick's work deals to a large extent with the mediumship of Emma Deane, a British psychic famed for her ability to produce photographs of the dead under conditions excluding fraud. It was the same Mrs. Deane

Photo 1 Hans Holzer supervising experiment of John Myers psychic photography

Photo 3 Holzer opening bag of chemicals

Photo 2 Holzer pans for developer and fixative

*Photos 4 and 5 Holz-
er's aunt Irma D.*

22

who was once visited by John Myers, then a novice in the field. He came merely to have a "sitting," like everybody else who sought out the elderly lady, and, for a few pennies, was photographed in her presence. Frequently Myers was to discover afterward the portrait of a dead loved one near him on the plate! To his surprise Mrs. Deane told him that some day soon he would be taking her place. Myers smiled incredulously and walked out. But when Mrs. Deane's health failed some time later, Myers, who had since discovered his own psychic and photographic powers, did indeed take over her studio.

I met John Myers in New York in 1959 because I had heard of his special psychic talents and was anxious to test him. Myers, at that point, was a man of independent means, a successful industrialist and well-known philanthropist who could not possibly gain anything from exposing himself to psychic research. But he also felt he owed something to his benefactors on "the other side of life," as the spiritualists call it, and for that reason he agreed to meet me. This indebtedness went back many years to when he was a dental surgeon in London, already aware of his psychic abilities and practicing two of his special crafts as sidelines. These were psychic photography – later a full-time occupation – and psychic healing. As a healer, he managed to help Laurence Parish, a wealthy American businessman, regain his eyesight where orthodox doctors had failed. In gratitude Parish offered Myers a position in his company in New York. At the time Myers was not making too much money, since he charged only a few pennies for each psychic photograph he took, and nothing for his healing work. He felt that the opportunity to go to America was being sent his way so that he might be useful in his new career *and* as a psychic, so he accepted.

In New York Myers proved himself a good asset to the company and eventually he rose to become its vice president, second only to the head of the company. Because of his new duties Myers now pursued his psychic work on only a sporadic basis, but behind the scenes he often backed other psychics or sponsored spiritualistic meetings that could not have found a hall were it not for Myers' financial support. He himself continued his activities as a psychic healer, however. Occasionally Myers agreed to tests, but only when important scientists or newspaper reporters were to be present. What Myers could no longer do in amount of work he made up for by the sheer power of observers' rosters.

I tested Myers' abilities as a psychic photographer on several occasions. At no time did he try to influence me in any way, or suggest anything, except that he was a sensitive man who resents being insulted. On one occasion I managed to persuade him to give a second public demonstration of his psychic photography on television. Since the first TV test in 1961 was, to my mind, very impressive, I felt another such test might prove valuable also. The program that had requested this test was the American Broadcasting Company's late night show emceed by Les Crane. This brash young man had on a previous occasion proved himself to me to be without sympathy toward psychic research, but I was there to protect Myers from any unpleasant remarks. We had brought the usual chemicals, all open to examination, and the program's producer had provided the photographic paper to be exposed; that is, they had it ready. But the moment never came. They had booked too many "acts" on this particular occasion, and time ran out before Myers and I could undertake the test. For over two hours Myers sat waiting quietly in the wings. But the little people who were in charge failed to understand the significance of Myers' willingness to do this experiment, and so he went home.

My first meeting with Myers in 1959 was followed by a sitting which was arranged for the purpose of demonstrating his abilities as a psychic photographer. This was in late July, and I set up the following test conditions: Myers was to accompany me on the afternoon of the planned sitting to a photographic supply store of my choice, where I would select and purchase the light-sensitive paper he required. Myers asked the clerk for ordinary developing paper. There are many types, of varying light-sensitivity, and Myers picked a medium-fast paper. The clerk brought the package of paper and I satisfied myself that it was from a fresh batch of materials, properly sealed and in no way damaged or tampered with. I then placed my signature across all corners of the outer envelope, and Myers did the same. The reason for Myers' insistence that he too should be allowed to place his own safeguards on the package goes back many years. When still a young man in England gaining a reputation as a psychic photographer, Myers was challenged to a test by a journalist named Lord Donegal. Not content to look for possible fraud by Myers, Donegal wanted to make sure he *would* be able to find some. Rather than take his chance that Myers might be honest, Donegal switched plates on him and thus produced a foolproof "fraud" – marked plates he himself had supplied. Naturally, Myers was accused publicly, and it took years of hard work to undo the damage. In the end, tiring of the joke, Donegal admitted his deeds. But the incident had turned Myers from a friendly, openhearted man into a cautious, suspicious person, who never quite trusted any experimenter fully.

For this reason, Myers wanted his signature on the package next to mine, so that he too could be sure I had not been tampering with the package. As soon as the bill for the paper was paid, I took the package and put it safely into my pocket. At no time did Myers hold it in his hands. We parted company and I went home, the package still in my possession. After dinner I went to Myers' apartment, where he and five other witnesses were already present. One of these was a photographer named Charles Hagedorn, a skeptic, and one was Myers' legal advisor, Jacob Gerstein, an attorney well known in business circles for his integrity and keen observation. Also present was the late Danton Walker, Broadway columnist of the *Daily News*, himself psychic and keenly interested in the subject, but by no means sure of its implications. None of the observers were "believers" as the term is usually used, but rather all were enlightened witnesses who were willing to accept unusual facts if they could be proven to them.

We entered a medium-sized room in which there was a table surrounded by four chairs, with additional chairs in the four corners. The only illumination came from a yellow overhead bulb, but the light was strong enough to read by without difficulty. The corners of the room were somewhat darker. Myers sat down on a chair in the left-hand corner, placed his hands over his eyes and went into a trance. I took the photographic paper out of my pocket, where it had been all this time, and placed it on the table in plain view of everyone present. At no time had Myers or anyone else among the guests "brushed past" me, or jostled me – a typical means of switching packages. Whenever I have the misfortune of sharing a microphone with a professional conjurer, this is one of his "explanations" of how the psychic phenomena must have been accomplished. I am, of course, familiar with many tricks of magic and always look out for them, but nothing of the sort was attempted. The package was still sealed, exactly as it had been all afternoon. After about five minutes Myers breathed deeply and opened his eyes, saying with a somewhat tired voice, "The paper is now exposed. You can open the package." With that, Walker and I proceeded to tear open the outer envelope, then the package of light-sensitive paper itself, and quickly threw the 20 sheets contained in it into the developing liquid we had also brought along. As soon as the sheets hit the liquid, various things happened to them that really should not have, if this had not been a psychice experiment

Unexposed photographic paper should show uniform results when exposed to a 60-watt yellow light and then developed. But here different things happened with each and every sheet! Some were totally blank. Others had forms on them, and some showed human faces. A few showed symbols, such as a tombstone, a tablet, a cross. As rapidly as we could we worked over the whole pack. Walker pulled out the sheets and threw them into the developer. I pulled them from the latter and into the fixative solution and out into clear water. Myers was still on his chair in the corner. We then put all the papers on a big towel to dry, and turned on all the lights in the room. Without touching any of the prints, we started to examine the results of Myers' psychic mediumship.

Clearly, if faces or figures appeared on these papers, fraud could not be the cause. One of the intriguing aspects of such an experiment is to hope for a likeness of someone one knew in physical life. Of course you never know *who* might turn up. Those who experiment or investigate psychic channels of various kinds, and anxiously hope for a specific loved one to make an entrance, are almost invariably disappointed. The genuine result of these experiments is quite unpredictable, as well it should be. So it was with considerable glee that I discovered among the faces a familiar one. As soon as the paper was completely dry I took it over to a strong light to make sure I was not guilty of wishful thinking. No, there was no mistake about it. Before me was a portrait of an aunt of mine, not particularly close, but someone I once knew well. Her name was Irma D. She had lived in Czechoslovakia and had fallen victim to the war. Exactly where or when she died we still do not know, for she, along with thousands of others, just disappeared under the Nazi occupation of her homeland. I found out about her sad end in 1945, when communications were restored with Europe. But this was 1959, and I really had not thought of her for many years. So it was with surprise that I found this sign of life, if you will, from a relative. Of course I went to my family album on returning home, to make sure it was she. I did not have the identical picture, but I had a group photograph taken more or less about the same period of her life. In this group shot, Irma is the girl on the right. The one on the left is my late mother, and the one in the middle a mutual school friend of both girls. This was taken when both sisters were still single; the psychic face, however, dates to her early years of marriage, a period one might think she would have considered her best and happiest years.

I took the psychic likeness and presented it to my father, a total skeptic at that time, without telling him anything about it. Instantly he recognized his late sister-in-law. I tested various other relatives, and the results were the same. I was so intrigued with all this that I implored Myers to give us another sitting immediately. He acceded to my request and on August 6, 1959, we met again at Myers' apartment. This time photographic film rather than paper was to be used, and a camera was brought into the room. The camera itself was a bellows type using 120-size film, and there was nothing unusual about its appearance. Myers used cut film rather than roll film, and the bellows seemed to be in perfect condition when I examined the camera. But there is romance connected with the history of this old camera. It used to belong to the celebrated British psychic photographers William Hope and, later, Mrs. Deane, and passed into Myers' hands in 1930, coming with him to America five years later.

Again present were the photographer Hagedorn and attorney Gerstein, along with two ladies, Gail Benedict, a publicist, and Mrs. Riccardi, an astrologer and artist. Hagedorn and Gerstein had bought the film at Kodak in New York, and the materials were in Hagedorn's possession until the moment when he and Gerstein loaded the camera in full view of the two ladies and myself. Farther back in the apartment, a group of about ten other persons watched the entire experiment, without taking part in it. It took somewhat longer to develop the exposed film than the paper of the first experiment, but again strange "extras" appeared on the film. In addition, the paper experiment was repeated and several faces appeared on the sheets, none of them, however, known to me or identified. This is not surprisisng, as psychic photography mediums are rare and the number of persons wishing to communicate from "over there" is presumably very great. For what is more vital than to let those left behind know that life does go on? I kept in touch with Myers after this experiment, but we did not try our hands again at it for some time.

One day in 1960 I visited his office and he told me of some pictures he had recently taken by himself. I realized that these were not as valid as those taken under my eyes, but it seemed to me rather ludicrous to assume that Myers would spend an evening trying to defraud himself! So I asked to be shown the pictures. Strangely, Myers felt compelled to show me but one of the pictures. I blanched when I looked at it. Though not as sharp as an "ordinary" photograph, the portrait was clearly that of a dear young friend of mine who had died unhappily not long before. At no time had I discussed her with Myers, nor had Myers ever met her in life. To be doubly sure I showed the picture to the young lady's mother and found her agreeing with me. At various seances and sittings this girl had made her presence known to me, often through strange mediums who did not even know my name or who had never met me until then. So it did not exactly come as a shock to see this further proof of continued desire to communicate.

It was not untill the summer of 1961 that Myers and I again discussed a maor experiment. PM East, produced then by channel 5 New York, came to me with a request to put together a "package"of psychic experiments. I decided to include Myers and his psychic photoraphy prominently .It was not easy to convince him to step into this kind of limelight, with all its limitations and pressures, but in the end he agreed to come. We made our conditions known, and Mike Wallace accepted them on behalf of the show. Wallace, a total skeptic, was to purchase ordinary photographic paper in a shop of his own choice and keep it on his person until air time. This he did, and the sealed, untampered-with paper was produced by him when the three of us went on camera. The developing and fixation liquids as well as the bowls were also supplied by the studio. Myers waited patiently in the wings while other segments of the program were telecast. All this time Wallace had the paper and liquids under his control. Finally we proceeded to take our seats onstage, with Myers on my left and Wallace on my right, perched on wooden stools without backs. The sole source of light now was an overhead yellow bulb, 60 watts in strength, and all the studio lights were turned off.

Immediately upon being on camera, the experiment began. When Wallace opened the package of sealed papers, and threw them one by one into the first liquid, immediately forms started to appear where no forms should appear, as we were dealing with totally virgin photographic paper. If by some freak condition these papers could have been exposed, then they should at the very least have appeared identical. This, however, was not the case. Several were totally blank, while others showed amorphous shapes and figures, one a human arm, one a head and one an as yet indistinct face. At this point a commercial made continuation of the experiment impossible, and the results were less than conclusive as far as the television audience was concerned. Something had, of course, appeared on the unexposed papers, but what? After the show I examined the dried prints carefully. One of them clearly showed a very fine portrait of my late mother, who had died exactly four years before the experiment took place. Now I had not thought of having my late mother put in an appearance, so to speak, to convince the skeptics of survival, nor had Myers any access to my family album. In fact Myers did not know that my mother had passed away.

Certainly Wallace did not manufacture this picture, for he was a firm nonbeliever in the possibility of personal survival. And I, as the researcher, certainly would know better than to produce a fake picture of my own mother if I intended to put over a trick. If anyone's mother, then Wallace's or Myers', certainly not my own, when I was the one person wo did have access to a likeness of my mother! The fact that the portrait which thus appeared is that of my late mother is less important than the fact that *any* face appeared at all, for even *that* is paranormal. Even if Myers had wanted to forge this psychic photograph, he would not have been able to do so. The picture of my mother in the family album is not accessible and had to be searched out from storage by me in order to match it up with the psychic image. I also had the negative stored away. The similarity is striking, notably the form of the nose and the parting of the hair; but there is a certain *glow* about the psychic photograph that is not present in the portrait made during her lifetime. The white, cottonlike substance surrounding the face is what I call a "matrix," made up from substance drawn from Myers' body in some fashion and, in my opinion, superimposed on the light-sensitive paper, thus making it, in addition, *psychically* sensitive. On this "film upon a film," then, a thought form of my later mother was imbedded, very much like a wire photo, except that the machine that made this possible was Myers' *body*.

Controlled experiments of this kind have established that communications from the so-called dead can indeed be received under conditions excluding any form of fraud, delusion or self-delusion. Needless, perhaps, to add that no financial rewards wahtever were involved for Myers in this experiment.

My next session with Myers came about as a result of United Press reporter Pat Davis' interest in the subject. I asked Myers that we try another experiment, and he agreed to do so on April 25, 1964. On this occasion the photographic paper was purchased by a trio of outsiders, Dr. S. A. Bell, a dentist, a lady associate of the doctor's, and Miss Lee Perkins of New York City. They accompanied Myers to a store of their own selection, where the paper was bought and initialed by them in the usual manner. Myers never touched the package. Three packages had been bought from a batch of photographic paper, presumed to be identical in all respects. The initialed three packages were then placed in a large envelope and the envelope sealed and stapled in the presence of attorney Gerstein. Gerstein then took charge of the paper and kept it with him until that evening when he brought it to the Myers apartment for the experiment.

In full view of all those present – about a dozen observers unfamiliar with the subject matter, plus Miss Davis and myself – Gerstein placed the three packages on the table and brought out three basins filled with developing and fixation liquids and water. Pat Davis, who had never met Myers until then, now stepped forward and, on Myers' suggestion, picked one of the three packages, which again was examined by Gerstein and me carefully as to possible violations. There were none. Miss Davis then opened the package and, one by one, placed the photographic paper sheets contained in it onto the first pan. All this was in full electric light, with the observers standing close by around the table.

HOW THIS PICTURE WAS OBTAINED

Date:

September 1961, 8 P.M.

Place:

On the air, during PM East, Channel 5, New York, a television program moderated by Mike Wallace.

Light conditions:

Total darkness in the studio except for one overhead 60-watt yellow bulb, at a distance of about 20 inches.

Camera:

No camera used.

Film:

No film, but ordinary photographic printing paper (so-called gaslight paper), purchased independently by Wallace at a shop of his own selection and kept sealed until air time.

Exposure:

Immediately upon opening package of unexposed photographic paper, each sheet was immersed in developer individually by Wallace, then transferred by him to hypo for fixation of obtained images. At no time did medium John Myers or Hans Holzer touch photographic papers until after they had been covered by various impressions which could not be accounted for by ordinary means of exposure. Each sheet was exposed to yellow light for the short time it took Wallace's hands to move the sheet from the package to the liquid.

Operator:

Wallace, in the presence of Holzer and to the left, photographic medium Myers, a dental surgeon and industrialist from London.

30

Photo 6 Psychic photograph of Holzer's mother.

Photo 6B Photograph of Holzer's mother from the family album.

As soon as the sheets touched the first liquid, forms and faces began to appear on them, varying from sheet to sheet. Among them was a clear likeness of the late Frank Navroth, immediately identified by Gerstein, who knew this man before his death. Another photograph was that of a young girl who had passed on five or six years ago and was identified by one of the observers present, Dan Kriger, an oil executive. Several people recognized the likeness of the late Congressman Adolph Sabath also. Pat Davis then requested that Myers leave the room so that we could determine whether his bodily nearness had any influence on the outcome of the experiment. Myers agreed and went to another part of the apartment. Pat Davis then took the second of the packages and opened it and again submerged the sheets in it exactly as she had done with the first package. Nothing happened. All sheets were blank and exactly alike, a little fogged from the exposure to the strong room light, but without any distinguishing marks whatever. She then opened the third and last package and did the same. Again nothing appeared on the sheets. Finally we used a few sheets still remaining in the first package, and again the results were negative as long as Myers was not within the same room.

III
AUTHENTIC "SPIRIT PICTURES" TAKEN AT SEANCES

Myers was not the only reputable psychic photography medium. For many years I worked with New Yorker Betty Ritter in cases involving her major talents as a clairvoyant. She is a medium who supplies valid information from the so-called dead and predicts events before they become objective reality. In this area Betty Ritter was excellent. She also developed her psychic photography to a point where it deserves to be taken very seriously.

Miss Ritter was a middle-aged woman of Italian descent, a pensioner who lived quietly and occasionally saw friends of friends who wanted a professional "reading" or a psychic consultation. She was a sincere spiritualist and also a devoted Catholic. Any thought of fraud or commercialism was completely alien to her character, and she remained a person of very modest circumstances. On the occasions when I requested photographic prints of her negatives she would not even ask for her own expenses.

From about 1955 on, Betty Ritter obtained unusual photographs with her old-fashioned bellows camera, results that came as much as a surprise to her as to the people she photographed. She was guided by an intuitive feeling that she should photograph the audiences where psychic energies might be present, perhaps as a result of large-scale production of thought forms, prayers, and other man-made force fields. She took her camera with her whenever going to a spiritualist church or meeting, or when sitting privately with people

Photo 7 Bettty Ritter photograph showing ectoplastic manifestations.

HOW THIS PICTURE WAS OBTAINED

Date:

1955. Evening.

Place:

Reverend Boyd's spiritualist church in New York City, during a quasi-public demonstration of Reverend M. Heaney.

Light conditions:

Normal room light (artificial). No strong reflectors of any kind.

Camera:

Old-type bellows camera (Kodak), size 116.

Film:

Kodak, medium-fast film.

Exposure:

1/25 second.

Operator:

Betty Ritter.

Developing and printing:

Local photography shop.

whom she knew well enough to be relaxed with. I often examined her camera and found it in perfect working order. She used standard firm and average developing laboratories. Many years later, she finally learned to print from her negatives, although she did not develop them herself. By no means was Betty Ritter a photographic technician. Some of the many pictures I have in my files that were taken by her, were snapped in my presence, others under conditions I consider satisfactory. I have selected four outstanding photographs from them, although each photograph is merely one of several similar ones obtained on the same roll of film and under similar conditions.

Both the medium and I considered the white lines to the left and the round ball on the right in Photo 7 to be concentrations of psychic energy. They cannot be explained by any kind of faulty equipment or materials. Pictures of this type are not too rare, and there seems to be a connection between the number of persons present in the room and the intensity of the phenomena. If ectoplasm is a substance drawn from the bodies of emotionally stimulated sitters, and I think it is, then this substance must assemble in some form or shape before it can be utilized via thought direction to perform some intelligent task. I think these streaks, known as "rods," are the raw materials that are used also in materializations of the dead, when these are genuine phenomena, and in poltergeist cases, when objects seemingly move of their own volition. This material, isolated some years ago in London and found to be a moist, smelly whitish substance related to albumen, undoubtedly comes from the body glands of the medium and her sitters or helpers. It is later returned to the sources, or that portion of it not used up at the end of the seance. It can be molded like wax into any form or shape. Strange as this may sound, it is thought direction that does the molding.

In the case of the spiritualist seance picture, no such molding took place, and what we see on the picture is merely the free ectoplasm as it is manufactured and assembled. The naked eye does not normally see this, of course. But then the human eye does not register much of the spectrum, either. The combination of sensitive camera and sensitive photographer or operator seems to be the catalyst to put this material onto photographic film. Just how this works we do not know fully, but it happens frequently under similar conditions and in all such cases faulty materials or cameras have been ruled out.

In Photo 2, we see how the ectoplasm can be used to bring home a definite message or thought form.

One of those present at this small gathering in Reverend Boyd's church was Helen M., whose father had died seven years before. He

Photo 8 Betty Ritter, self-por-
trait,1951. Energy "ball" above head

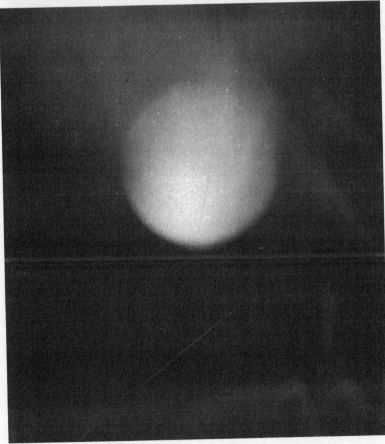

Photo 9 Private sitter photographed by Ritter eclipsed
by psychic energy "ball" and
beginning formation of a figure

35

had lost a leg in his physical life. The communicator, through the medium, wanted to prove his identity in some form and proposed to show his severed leg as a kind of signature, while at the same time making a point of his having two good legs once more in *his* world.

On the print (which matches the negative which I have seen) the white substance of the "new" leg is superimposed on the leg of the sitter. There appear to be two extra hands in the picture, while the rest of the photograph is sharp, pointing to supernormal origin of the extras rather than conventional double exposure – the rest of the picture is sharply defined. It is my opinion that ectoplasm was molded via thought into the desired shapes and the latter then made capable of being photographed.

As the psychic photographer develops his or her skill, the extras become more sophisticated until they eventually are faces or entire figures. With Betty Ritter it started with concentrations of power or ectoplasm, and later included such higher forms of imagery as hands, a cross symbol and, eventually, writing. Photo #13 came about in the following manner: In 1965 I had recommended a young lady named Trudy S. to Betty. I had unsuccessfully tried to break the hold a dead person evidently had on her. This was probably due to the fact that Trudy herself is psychic and therefore supplies the desired entrance way. The attentions of this young man, who died in a car accident and had been a friend of the young girl's during his lifetime, were not welcomed by Miss S. after his death. I thought that perhaps Betty Ritter, being a strong medium (which I decidedly am not), might be able to "outdraw" the unwelcome intruder and, as it turned out, I was right in my suggestion.

During the time when Trudy S. went to see Betty Ritter to break the hold of the dead man, she also had a boyfriend in her physical world. But the intruder from beyond the veil kept interfering until the couple broke up, largely because of the situation. On March 3, 1965, Trudy S. had a sitting with Betty during which Betty took some photographs. On one of them, imbedded in the well-known "cotton wool" of psychic photography, there appears the word ROME in black letters. Nothing in the negative, the camera, the film or the paper can account for this writing. Why ROME? At the time of the sitting Trudy's boyfriend was in Italy and on his way to Rome. Was Betty's camera catching a thought form from Trudy's uncon -

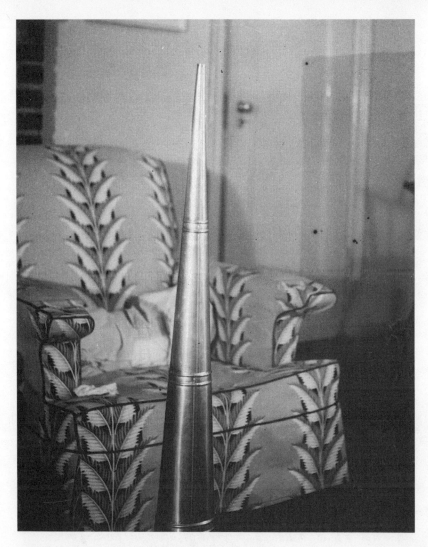

Photo 12 Hans and Catherine Holzer sitting at Ritter's apartment. Notice figure forming behind the couple and "extra" arm trying to reach out to Holzer. Holzer recognized the arm as that of his late mother's. Catherine was pregnant at the time (May 10, 1963) with their first daughter, Nadine, and this perhaps explains the reason for Holser's mother's contact and concern.

Photo 13 Holzer's deceased mother extending an arm to the couple.

Photo 14 One-legged communicator showing ectoplastic leg superimposed on medium as means of identification in this Betty Ritter photograph

HOW THIS PICTURE WAS OBTAINED

Date:

February 11, 1963.

Place:

Reverend Boy'd spiritualist church in New York City.

Ligyht conditions:

Normal room light.

Camera:

Kodak roll film camera, bellows, size 116.

Film:

Medium-fast black-and-white Kodak 116.

Exposure:

1/25 second.

Operator:

Betty Ritter.

Developing and printing:

Local photography shop.

HOW THIS PICTURE
WAS OBTAINED

Date:

March 3, 1965.

Place:

Betty Ritter's apartment,
New York.

Light conditions:

Ordinary room light.

Camera:

Old-style Kodak bellows
camera, size 116.

Film:

Medium-fast black-and-
white Kodak 116.

Exposure:

1/25 second.

Operator:

Betty Ritter.

**Developing and
printing:**

Local photography shop.

Photo 15 "ROME" in ectoplastic "cloud" in upper left on psychic photo taken by Betty Ritter
with sitter Trudy S. in 1965.

IV
SPIRIT PHOTOGRAPHY
AT A CAMP

Spiritualist camps have been the subject of much controversy and investigation as to their honesty, and are best, a mixed bag of evidence. Years ago the late Eileen Garrett commissioned me to look into fake materializations at some of the camps. I found many of the resident psychic readers at these camps to be honest and the number of fraudulent cases small. Nevertheless, they do happen and one must guard against being too trusting when visiting these places.

Maggy Conn was a well-known newspaper columnist for a string of Eastern newspapers. In February 1982 she asked me to examine a picture taken in 1947 at Camp Silverbelle, in Ephrata, Pennsylvania.

While neither Maggy nor I know who the manifesting spirit in the photograph is, it does appear to match in texture and general appearance the kind of spirit pictures taken under test conditions, so I have no reason to doubt it. Maggie is on the right, and the second picture shows how she looked in 1972.

Photo 16 Psychic photograph of Maggie Conn

Photo 17 1972 Portrait photograph of Maggie Conn

V
THE "BABY DOLL" SPIRIT

I am indebted to Nancy Stallings of the Maryland Society for Parapsychology, along with her co-investigator and husband, Ron, for the following bizarre case of spirit communication. Despite its "off the wall" aspects, so to speak, I have no cause to doubt the veracity of the account.

The report regarding this incident, addressed to the Stallings, was dated September 23, 1980. Monica Rovecamp was in Franklin Square Hospital near Baltimore, giving birth to the couple's first daughter. On September 14, around noon, Mr. Rovecamp took some pictures of his wife and their newborn child with a standard 35mm camera and ordinary color print film. A nurse suggested she take one of the couple with the baby.

When the film came back from the lab, there appeared on the wall behind the family a tiny baby-like figure which they dubbed "baby doll." The trouble with this very clear image was that nothing like it was on the wall behind them. Mrs. Rovecamp asked the nurse who had taken the photograph to check the room where the picture was taken to see whether there was any kind of painting or decoration on the wall behind the bed. There was not.

There is considerable controversy as to when the Spirit or soul enters the body. I have never encountered a similar phenomenon.

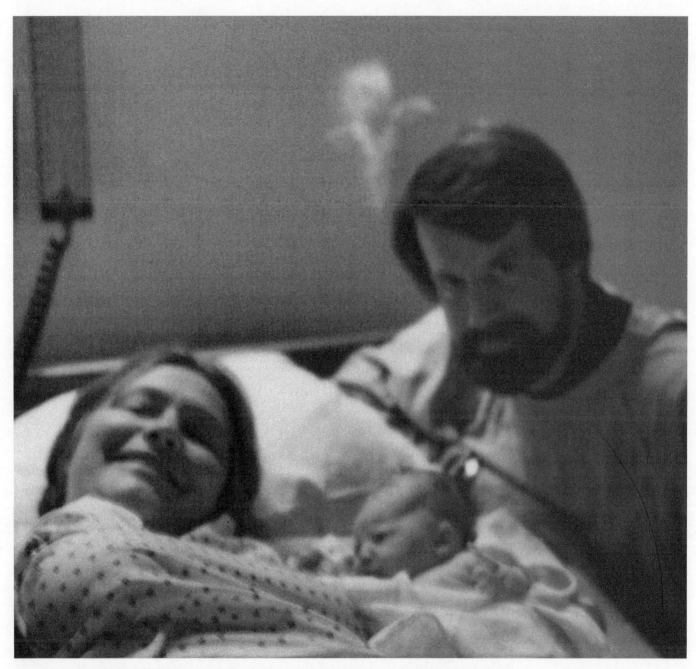

Photo 18 The "Baby Doll" Spirit

VI
SOME UNEXPECTED
SPIRIT FACES

Mary Krauss of Boston, Massachusetts, contacted me in late September 1972 because of an odd spirit picture she had taken.

The little boy holding the cat in this picture, taken in October 1965 in Pearl River, New York, is apparently quite unaware of any "presence," but the cat evidently is not, as she stares, not into the camera or at the photographer, but at "something" she can see to the left of the boy, which neither he nor the photographer could see.

The swirling white mass on the lower right of the picture contains two faintly visible faces, which Mrs. Krauss circled. At the time, only the little boy, Krauss' brother and Mrs. Krauss herself were in the room with the cat.. But whose face or faces is it?

Shortly after Mrs. Krauss' family moved into the house, it became clear that they were not alone though they could not actually see a presence. On cleaning out the attic, however, they noticed that objects had been moved about, and sensed a strong presence in the area. It was in the attic that the picture was taken. Could it be the previous occupant wanted to manifest his or her continued presence in the house?

Photo 19 The unexpected face

VII
PHOTOGRAPHING
MATERIALIZATIONS

Born in Westphalia in 1911, Hanna Hamilton was always "unusual" to her family. She had an uncanny (but uncontrollable) ability to produce psychic photographs.

In early August 1977 Miss Hamilton attempted to take a photograph of her living room towad her outdoor garden. Only Hanna and her cats were in the room at the time. Picture her surprise when a whitish female body (Hamilton called her "the streaker") appeared in the picture. But what appears to be a nude is really a white materialization made of ectoplasm.

Hamilton had no idea who the visitor was, but with so many "spirit friends" in her earthly life, it might have been anyone's guess.

Photo 20 Hanna Hamilton's psychic photograph

**HOW THIS PICTURE
WAS OBTAINED**

Date:

August 1977.

Place:

Hanna Hamilton's cottage in Hollywood, California.

Light Conditions:

Daylight.

Camera:

Kodak pocket Instamatic 10.

Film:

Appropriate Kodak film.

Operator:

Hanna Hamilton.

Photo 21 Hanna Hamilton

Dixie Tomkins, a very religious lady in Troy, Michigan, contacted me regarding a series of unusual photographs taken in December 1968 during the christening of one of her children. Mrs. Tomkins had been psychic all her life, and the picture did not surprise her, but she turned to me for an explanation.

A materialized male figure appears in the picture, close to the baby, evidently watching the ceremony.

This also seems to show that such ectoplastic figures can be invisible to the naked eye but not to the camera. That is, if and when a psychic catalyst is present in close vicinity.

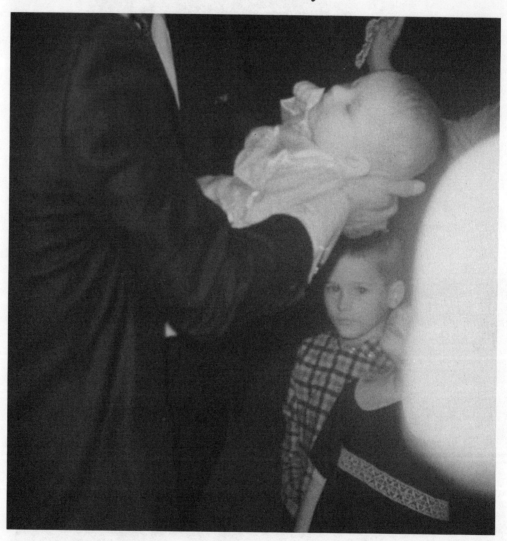

Photo 22 Dixie Tomkins' psychic photographs

Photo 23 Dixie Tomkins' psychic photograph

VIII
THE PHYSICIAN,
CATHERINE THE GREAT,
AND POLAROID
SPIRIT PHOTOGRAPHY

D r. Andrew von Salza, a West Coast physician originally without any interest in psychic matters, began to realize that he had a strange gift for psychic photography. He was a jolly and successful man with medical degrees from the Universities of Berlin and Tartu (Estonia). A leading rejuvenation specialist in California, he was nothing more than an amateur shutterbug without the slightest interest in anything supernormal or psychic. Unexpected and totally unwarranted "extras" have appeared on his photographs, both those taken with regular cameras and with the speedy Polaroid type. He had known of my interest in psychic research through a mutual friend, Gail Benedict, the public-relations director of the Savoy-Hilton, where he usually stayed. Although I had heard about his strange encounters with this subject, my only previous meeting with the doctor was on a social occasion, where others were present and when the chance to discuss the matter deeply did not present itself. At that time, too, von Salza met my ex-wife, Catherine, and was told that she was of Russian descent, to which he remarked that he was a Balt himself. But neither the doctor nor my wife went into any detailed history of her background.

Finally, in March 1966, von Salza arrived in New York on business and unexpectedly telephoned me, offering to experiment in my presence, as I had so long desired him to do. We arranged for a get-together at our house on Sunday, March 13, and I asked Gail Benedict to bring the doctor over. In addition, a friend of Miss Benedict's, Mrs. Marsha Slansky, a designer and not particularly experienced in matters of psychic research, joined us as an additional observer. Shortly after their arrival, the doctor suddenly requested that my wife seat herself in an armchair at the far end of the living room, because he felt the urge to take a picture of her. It was at this point that I examined the camera and film and satisfied myself that no fraud could have taken place.

The first picture taken showed a clear superimposition, next to my wife, of a female figure, made up of a white, semitransparent substance. As a trained historian I immediately recognized that as an attempted portrait of Catherine the Great. The sash of her order, which she liked to wear in many of her official portraits, stood out quite clearly on this print. We continued to expose the rest of the pack, and still another pack which I purchased at a corner drugstore a little later that evening, but the results were negative except for some strange light streaks which could not be accounted for normally. The doctor handed me the original picture, and the following day I had a laboratory try to make me a duplicate which I was to send him for the record. Unfortunately the results were poor, the sash did not show at all in the reproduction, and I was told that this was the best they could do because the original was a Polaroid picture and not as easily copied as an ordinary print. At any rate I mailed this poor copy to Andrew von Salza in San Francisco with my explanation and regrets. To my surprise we received a letter from him, dated March 25, 1966, in which he enclosed two pictures of the same subject. Only this time the figure of Catherine the Great was sharp and detailed, much more so than in the original picture and, in fact, superimposed on the whitish outline of the first photograph. The whole thing looked so patently fraudulent at first glance that I requested exact data on how this second "round" was taken. Not that I suspected the doctor of malpractice, but I am a researcher and cannot afford to be noble.

Von Salza obliged. When he had received my poor copy of his fine psychic picture, he had tacked it to a blank wall in a corner of his San Francisco apartment in order to rephotograph it. Why he did this he cannot explain, except that he felt "an urge" to do so. He used a Crown Graphic camera with Polaroid back, size 4 x 5, an enlarging lens opening of F/32, with the camera mounted on a tropod about a yard or less away from the subject. His exposure for the rephotographing experiment was one second by daylight plus one 150-watt lamp.

Furthermore, Dr. von Salza offered to repeat the experiment in my presence whenever I came to San Francisco. What struck me as remarkable about the whole business was of course the fact, unknown to the doctor, that my ex-wife Catherine is a direct sixth-generation descendant of Catherine the Great. This was not discussed with him until after the first picture was obtained. Nevertheless Gail Benedict reported that on the way over to our apartment, von Salza suddenly and cryptically asked, "Why do I keep thinking of Catherine the Great?" Now had he wanted to defraud us, surely he would not have tipped his hand in this manner. The two rephotographed pictures sent to me by the doctor are not identical; on one of them a crown appears over my ex-wife's head! Several psychics with whom my ex-wife and I have "sat," who knew nothing whatever about my ex-wife or her background, have remarked that they "saw" a royal personality protecting my wife. New York medium Betty Ritter even described her by name as Catherine. It is true also that my ex-wife has a strong interest in the historical Catherine, and finds herself drawn frequently to books dealing with the life of the Empress. Although her sisters and brothers are equally close in descent to the Russian ruler, they do not show any particular affinity toward her.

Photo 24 Dr. Andrew von Salza took this remarkable picture of Catherine Holzer in her home; white" extra" of Mrs. Holzer's direct ancestor Catherine of Russia on right.

Photo 25 Contemporary print of Catherine the Great showing similar sash of order; note also outstreched arm, contour of hairdo.

HOW THIS PICTURE
WAS OBTAINED.

Date:

March 13, 1966, 9 P.M.

Place:

The living room of Hans
and Catherine Holzer's
apartment, New York City.

Light conditions:

Ordinary room lights, all
shielded from reflection and
glare, occasional lamps, but
no overhead cciling lights.

Camera:

Polaroid 103, the "better"
model of the line.

Film:

Polaroid film pack, obtained
from photographic dealer
and examined by Holzer
prior to insertion in camera,
and found untouched.

Exposure:

1/100 second.

Operator:

Dr.. Andrew von Salza of
San Francisco, California.

Photo 26 Second impression of Catherine shows it similar to contemporary prints. This picture was produced under Holzer's control.

Photo 27 Note outstreched arm of Catherine holding crown. Taken in presence of investigator.

The whole matter of these pictures was so outlandish that I felt either they were clever frauds and that I was being duped (although I did not see how this was possible under my stringent conditions) or that the material had to be factual, appearances to the contrary. Circumstantial evidence can be very misleading in so controversial a subject as psychic photography and I was determined not to allow opinions, pro or con, to influence my findings in this case.

Consequently, I went to San Francisco in May 1966, to test the good doctor. In my presence he took the original picture and mounted it on the wall, then placed film into his Crown Graphic camera with a Polaroid back. I inspected camera and film and nothing had been tampered with. The first two pictures yielded results; again a clear imprint of Cathering the Great was superimposed on the whitish outline of the original. But this time Catherine extended an arm toward her descendant! In her extended right hand the Empress tendered a crown to my ex-wife, but the two pictures are otherwise somewhat different in detail and intensity, although taken one after the other under identical light and exposure conditions *in my presence*. At this point I confess I became somewhat impatient and said aloud, "I wish Catherine would give us a message. What is she trying to tell us?" As if I had committed *l'ese majestè*, the psychic camera fell silent; the next picture showed nothing further than the whitish outline. We discontinued the experiment at this point. I inspected the camera once more and then left the doctor.

Before we parted I once more inspected the camera. It looked just like any ordinary Crown Graphic does, except for the Polaroid back. The enlarging lens was still set at F/32; the exposure, I knew, had been just one second, using ordinary daylight reinforced by one 150-watt lamp. Dr. von Salza later sent me a cheerful note in which he said, "Seeing is believing, but even seeing, so many cannot believe, including myself." He found the whole situation very amusing and made no serious effort to do much about it scientifically, except that he did cooperate with me whenever I asked him to.

Von Salza's first encounter with the uncanny was in 1963, when the widow of a colleague of his, Dr. Benjamin Sweetland, asked him to do a photo portrait of her. Von Salza obliged, but imagine their surprise when the face of the late husband appeared superimposed on a lampshade in the room. No double exposure, no fraud, no rational explanation for this phenomenon could be found, although von Salza, with his worldly training, insisted that "there had to be some other explanation!" To test this situation, he decided to photograph the widow Sweetland again, but with another camera and outdoors.

Using a Leica and color film, and making sure that all was in order, he found to his amazement that one of the 20 exposures showed the late doctor's face against the sky.

Dismissing the whole incident for want of an explanation and trying his best to forget it, he was again surprised when another incident took place. This time he was merely using up the last picture in his roll, shooting at random against the wall of his own room. When the roll was developed, there appeared on the wall the face of a young girl that had not been there when he took the picture. He was upset by this and found himself discussing the matter with a friend and patient of his by the name of Mrs. Pierson. She asked to be shown the picture. On inspection, she blanched. Andrew von Salza had somehow photographed the face of her "dead" young daughter. Although the doctor knew of the girl's untimely death, he had never seen her in life.

Several more incidents of this nature convinced the doctor that he had somehow stumbled onto a very special talent, like it or not. He began to investigate the subject to find out if others also had his kind of "problems." Among the people interested in psychic phenomena in the San Francisco area was Evelyn Nielsen, with whom von Salza later shared a number of experiments. He soon discovered that her presence increased the incidence rate of psychic "extras" on his exposures, although Miss Nielsen herself never took a psychic photograph without von Salza's presence, proving that it was he who was the mainspring of the phenomenon.

I have examined these photographs and am satisfied that fraud is out of the question for a number of reasons, chiefly technical, since most of them were taken with Polaroid cameras and developed on the spot before competent witnesses, including myself.

One day in New York City, Mrs. Pierson, who had been intrigued by the psychic world for a number of years, took Dr. von Salza with her when she visited the famed clairvoyant Carolyn Chapman.

Dr. von Salza had never heard of the lady, since he had never been interested in mediums. Mrs. Pierson had with her a Polaroid color camera. Von Salza offered to take some snapshots of Mrs. Chapman as souvenirs.

Imagine everybody's surprise when Mrs. Chapman's grandfather appeared on one of the pictures. Von Salza had no knowledge of what the old man looked like nor had he access to any of his photographs, since he did not know where he was going that afternoon in New York.

Another time, a friend of von Salza's, Dr. Logan, accompanied him, Mrs. Pierson, and Evelyn Nielsen to Mount Rushmore, where the group photographed the famous monument of America's greatest presidents. To their utter amazement, there was another face in the picture – Kennedy's!

Dr. Logan remained skeptical, so it was arranged that he should come to von Salza's house in San Francisco for an experiment in which he was to bring his own film.

First, he took some pictures with von Salza's camera and nothing special happened. Then von Salza tried Logan's camera and still there were no results. But when Dr. Logan took a picture of a corner in von Salza's apartment, using von Salza's camera, the result was different: on the Polaroid photograph there appeared in front of an "empty" wall a woman with a hand stretched out toward him. As Dr. von Salza reports it, the other doctor turned white —that woman had died only that very morning on his operating table!

In early May 1965 I went to San Francisco to observe the doctor at work–psychic photography work, that is, not his regular occupation, which is never open to anyone but the subjects! I fortified myself with the company of two "outsiders," my sister-in-law, Countess Marie Rose Buxhoeveden, and a friend, social worker Lori Wyn, who came with me to von Salza's apartment. There we met the doctor, Evelyn Nielsen and Mrs. Sweetland, as well as two other ladies, friends of the doctor's, who had been sympathetic to the subject at hand. It was late afternoon, and we all had dinner engagements, so we decided to get started right away.

With a sweeping gesture the doctor invited me to inspect the camera, already on its tripod facing the wall, or, as he called it, his "ghost corner," for he had always had best results by shooting away from the bright windows toward the darker portion of his big living room. The walls were bare except for an Indian wall decoration and a portrait of the doctor. In a way, they reminded me of motion-picture screens in their smoothness and blue-gray texture. But there was absolutely nothing on those walls that could be blamed for what eventually appeared "on" them.

I stepped up to the camera and looked inside, satisfying myself that nothing had been pasted in the bellows or gizmo, or on the lens. Then I looked at the film, which was an ordinary Polaroid film pack, black-and-white, and there was no evidence of its having been tampered with. The only way to do this, by the way, would have been to slit open the pack and insert extraneous matter into the individual

During San Francisco experiment with Dr. Andrew von Salza, several portrait "extras" appeared on Polaroid film. Others on couch are Evelyn Nielsen, associate, and Dr. von Salza and friends.

HOW THIS PICTURE WAS OBTAINED

Date:

May 1965, late afternoon, bright sun.

Place:

Apartment of Dr. Andrew von Salza, San Francisco, California.

Light conditions:

Daylight coming into the room.

Camera:

Crown Graphic with Polaroid film back, 4 x 5.

Film:

Polaroid black-and-white film, fast.

Exposure:

F/16, 1/250 second.

Operator:

Dr. von Salza.

Developing:

Instantaneous by von Salza in full view of witnesses.

Witnesses:

Evelyn Nielsen, Marie Rose Buxhoeveden, Lori Wynn, Mrs. Sweetland, two other laties and Hans Holzer.

Photo 28 Psychic photo taken in Holzer's presence by Dr. von Salza shows portrait of the elder Rockefeller in center.

pieces of film, something requiring great skill, total darkness and time. Even then traces of the cuttings would have to appear. The pack Dr. von Salza used was fresh and untouched.

The room was bright enough, as light streamed in from the windows opposite the L-shaped couch which lined the walls. The seven of us now sat down on the couch. Von Salza set the camera and exposed the first piece of film. Within sight of all of us, he developed the film in the usual fast Polaroid manner and then showed it to me. Over our heads there appear clearly four extra portraits, and the wall can be seen through them. I did not recognize any of the four in this instance. The doctor continued, this time including himself in the picture by presetting the camera and then taking his place next to Evelyn Nielsen on the couch.

The second picture, when developed, evoked some gasps of recognition from the audience. Four faces of various size appeared and a light-shaft (of psychic energy?) also was now evident on the left side of the photograph. But the gasp of recognition was due to the likeness of the late John D. Rockefeller, Sr. I might add here that this gentleman must have an avid interest in communicating with the world he left in 1937 at age 90. His face has appeared in other instances of psychic photography, especially in Britain with John Myers.

IX
VIVIEN LEIGH'S
POST-MORTEM PHOTOGRAPH

Although Sybil Leek, the British author, trance medium, and psychic, had done extraordinary things in my presence, notably fine trance work and clairvoyance, she never considered herself a photographic medium. On one or two occasions strange objects did appear on photographs taken of her or in her presence, but she had never pursued the matter.

On a Friday morning in July 1967, Sybil telephoned me in great agitation. She had just had a very vivid dream, or at any rate fallen into a state similar to the dream state. Someone named Vivien had communicated with her and remarked that she was now going on a holiday. Did I know any Vivien? Why me, I asked. Because this communicator wanted Sybil Leek to call me and tell me. Was there anything more? No, just that much. I pondered the matter. The only Vivien I ever knew personally was a young girl not likely to be on the Other Side as yet. But, of course, one never knows. I was still pondering the matter when the Saturday newspaper headlines proclaimed the death of Vivien Leigh. It appeared that she had just been discovered dead in her London apartment, but death might have come to her any time before Saturday, most likely on Friday. Suddenly I saw the connection and called Sybil. Did she know Vivien Leigh at all? She did indeed, although she had not seen her for some time. Years ago Vivien Leigh would consult Sybil Leek in personal matters, for Sybil was pretty good at sorting things out for her friends.

There was definitely a relationship. Nobody in the world knew that Vivien Leigh had died *on Friday*. The discovery was made on Saturday. And yet Sybil had her communication during Thursday night. The date? June 30, 1967. I felt it was the actress' way of saying goodbye and at the same time letting the world know that life continued. That was on Saturday. On Monday Sybil had a visitor at the Stewart Studios, where she usually stays when in New York. Her visitor, Edmond Hanrahan, was so impressed with the unusual decor of the studio that he decided to take some color pictures with his camera, which he happened to have with him at the time. The date was July 3, 1967. Several pictures were of Sybil Leek. There was nothing remarkable about any of them, except one. Partially obstructing Sybil is the face of a dark-haired woman with an unmistakable profile–that of Vivien Leigh!

Both Sybil and the photographer remember clearly that there was nobody else with them at the time, nor was there anything wrong with either film or camera. The psychic extra seems soft and out of focus, as if the figure had stepped between camera and Sybil, but too close to be fully in focus.

I questioned Mr. Hanrahan about the incident. He admitted that this was not the first time something or someone other than the person he was photographing showed up on a negative. On one particularly chilling occasion he had been photographing the widow of a man who had been murdered. On the negative the murdered man appeared next to his widow! Hanrahan used a Honeywell Pentax 35mm camera and Ektachrome film when he caught Vivien Leigh on film. He did not employ a flashgun but used all the available room light. He was relieved to hear that there was nothing wrong with his ability as a photographer or his camera, and he could not very well be held accountable for unseen models.

Date:

July 3, 1967. Afternoon

Place:

Stewart Studios, New York

Light conditions:

Room light, electric. No flash.

Camera:

Honeywell Pentax, 35mm

Film:

Ektachrome, artificial light (20 exposures).

Exposure:

1/50 second, open lens.

Operator:

Edmond Hanrahan.

Developing and printing:

Local photography shop (via Kodak).

Photo 29 British psychic Sybil Leek partially eclipsed by psychic photograph of erst while friend Vivien Leigh. Picture was taken by semi-professional photographer-YachtsmanEdmond Hanrahan about a week after star's death.

X
BETTY DYE'S
"PSYCHIC VIDEOS"

Betty Dye, a remarkable psychic healer with an excellent track record of accomplishment cures, many of them confirmed by medical professionals, is also a talented psychic medium. She followed up her success as a healer with experiments in psychic photography – and before she knew it, she was being besieged, unexpectedly, by large numbers of eager spirits wishing to communicate their continued existence "over there" by impressing their faces onto Betty's mind...and paper.

Mrs. Dye held ordinary index cards in her hands and allowed the restless ones to impress them through her mediumship. The portraits of the dead were faint, but they were clearly faces of individual people. Betty Dye then used a contemporary camera with a zoom lens to photograph the psychic cards and thus made the faces more visible.

And who are all these strangers? We don't know. Betty Dye sensed them to be "dead people" eager to communicate with the world of the living.

Date:

April 1978.

Place:

Betty Dye's home in
Stonewall, Georgia.

Light conditions:

Daylight.

Camera:

Standard contemporary
Japanese-made zoom cam-
era.

Film:

Black- and- White Kodak.

Operator:

Betty Dye.

Developing:

Local drugstore.

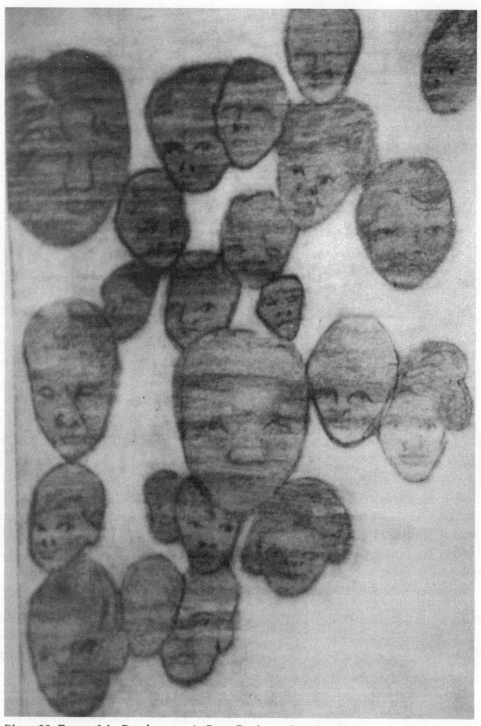

Photo 30 Faces of the Dead appear in Betty Dye's psychic pictures.

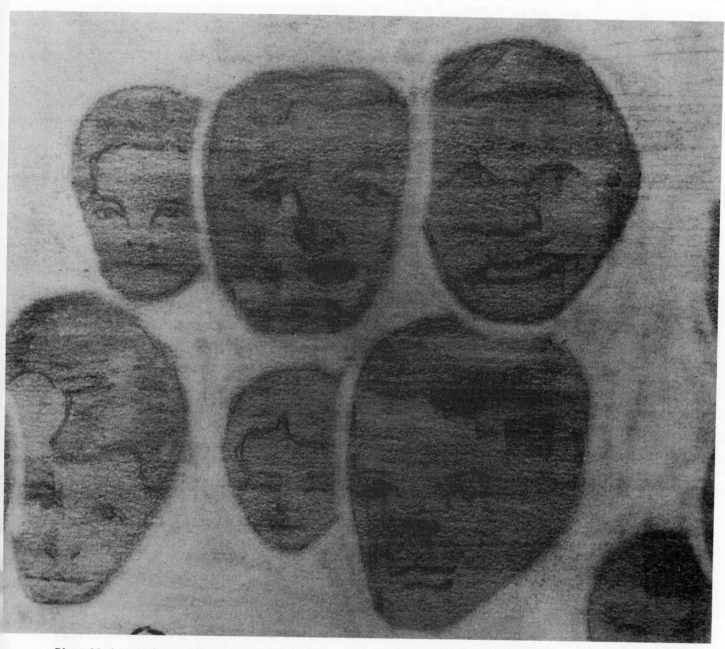

Photo 31 A second photo from Betty Dye's home.

XI
MAE BURROWS'
GHOSTLY FAMILY PICTURE

Mae Burrows has long since joined her family on "the other side of life." But for many years she was the undisputed premier medium in Cincinnati, Ohio, and her reputation as such, and a devout spiritualist, was similar to the celebrated mediums of turn-of-the- century England.

In 1930 a photographer friend visited Mrs. Burrows, and asked to photograph her with a plate camera, then the best way of taking photographs. She readily agreed to sit for him, and the result was indeed startling, though not so much to the medium as to the photographer.

Instead of getting just a nice portrait of his friend, the photographer captured images of a lot of "extras," as these psychic pictures are called.

First of all, there is the picture of Mrs. Burrow's Indian guide, and while investigators may have differing opinions about the prevalence of Indians among spirit guides (controls), the fact is, most professional mediums do have them, perhaps because Indian shamans were so close to being spiritualist mediums.

I saw Mrs. Burrows in 1970 and again in 1971, when she described the others in the remarkable photograph. There are three women in the picture, which she identified as her great-grandmother who died 75 years prior, her aunt who had been gone for 73 years, and her sister, who died 64 years before our meeting. As for the men, they were two medical doctors named Crowley and Ramey, and the man who turns his head sideways in the picture was a friend of the family who had taken his own life 76 years before.

Group spirit pictures like this are not so rare and have been obtained under strictest test conditions. There is no question as to the authenticity of this one.

Photo 32 *Mrs. Burrows psychic holograph.*

HOW THIS PICTURE
WAS OBTAINED

Date:

1930.

Place:

Mae Burrow's apartment in Cincinnati, Ohio.

Light condition:

Daylight.

Camera:

Plate camera of the period.

Operator:

Mae Burrow's photographer- friend.

XII
HOW THE
DEAD TEACHER
SAID GOOD-BYE

Evelyn England a busy professional portrait photographer in Los Angeles, California, had always known of her psychic gift but paid no attention to it. To her, this was simply part of life, and the supernatural was farthest from her mind.

Even as a youngster, England had ESP experiences, especially of the gift of finding lost objects under strange circumstances, as if driven by some inner voice. But despite these leanings she had no particular interest in the subject itself and merely took it for granted that others also had ESP.

One of England's jobs was photographing high-school yearbook pictures. So it was merely a routine assignment when she was called on to take the picture of Mr. G., a mathematics teacher. The date was Saturday, April 3, 1965. He was the last of the faculty to come in for his portrait. Her studio was closed on Sunday. On Monday England developed and retouched the print, and Tuesday morning she mailed it to the school. A few hours later she received a phone call from the school principal. Had Mr. G. come in for his sitting? Yes, Miss England answered, and informed the principal that the print was already in the mail. At this there was a slight pause. Then the principal explained that Mr. G. had died unexpectedly on Sunday.

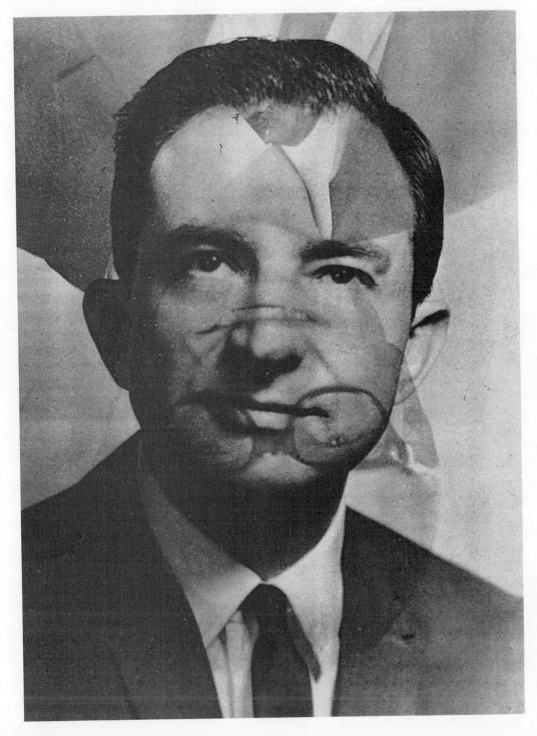

HOW THIS PICTURE
WAS OBTAINED

Date:

May 1965.

Place:

Evelyn England's photography studio, Los Angeles, California.

Light conditions:

Studio printing lights.

Camera:

A standard printer.

Paper:

Standard printing paper.

Operator:

Evel;yn England, professional commercial photographer

Photo 33 and 34 Professional commercial photographer Evelyn England accidentally produced psychic photo of dead client while developing another man's portrait.

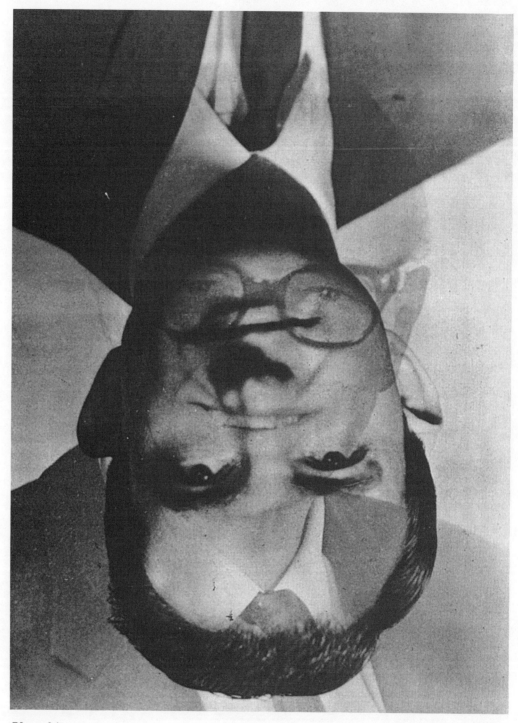

Photo 34

72

In May a Mr. H. came into her studio who remarked that he felt she had a good deal of ESP, being himself interested in such matters. Miss England took his portrait. He then came in to pick his choice from the proofs. When she placed the print into the developer, to her amazement, it was not Mr. H.'s face that came up – but Mr. G.'s, the dead mathematics teacher's face. A moment later, while she was still staring in disbelief, the portrait of her client Mr. H. came upon the same print, stronger than the first portrait and facing the opposite way from it.

Miss England was a very meticulous photographer.. She never left an undeveloped print around. She always developed each print fully, never leaving half-finished prints behind. No one but she used the studio. There was no "rational" explanation for what had happened. The smiling face of the late mathematics teacher was there to remind her that life was not over for him–or perhaps a token of gratitude for having been the last person to have seen him "alive." Hastily, Miss England printed another picture of Mr. H., and it was just a normal photograph.

Other "dead" persons later used her skills to manifest themselves, but this incident was the most remarkable one in her psychic life.

XIII
THE SEANCES WITH FLORENCE

Florence Sternfels, of Edgewater, New Jersey, was a nice, middle-class woman who had become famous as a "psychometrist" (a person who can touch an object belonging to someone and thereby learn facts about that person). She listed herself as a psychometrist in the local telephone book, and offered private readings to those who sought her out.

Early in our relationship, Florence Sternfels came to an investigative sitting of a group which met at the headquarters of the Association for Research and Enlightenment (Cayce Foundation) in New York City. The photographs presented here, taken in total darkness with infrared film, show contact being made by some entities, though the manifestations are only in their early stages.

Whenever Florence Íternfels referred to her unusual powers she called them simply "the forces." Not one to be very specific in scientific matters, the late psychometrist was in great awe of her own supernormal abilities and left the explanations to others. Not that she was not proud of her achievements. She did help the FBI on several occasions, and was a whiz at finding missing persons. She was not merely a very good "reader," a clairvoyant, but much more than that. Her body definitely had strange qualities. For one thing, she was able to put the telephone or the electric system in her house out of

HOW THESE PICTURES WERE OBTAINED

Date:

1952.

Place:

Association for Research and Enlightenment Headquarters, New York City.

Light conditions:

Total darkness, infrared film, black and white.

Exposure:

Time exposure, several seconds.

Camera:

Super Ikonta B, Zeiss.

Operator:

Hans Holzer.

Developing:

New York lab.

Photos 35 and 36 experimental photographic session with Florence

commission by merely touching it. She had to be very careful about this strange quirk of hers, because the telephone company saw nothing humorous in having to come time and again to fix the apparatus. So Florence had always someone–usually her brother, Nelson–to take care of mundane matters for her, while she did the psychic work.

My acquaintanceship with Florence went back many years. I met her through a study group interested in ESP research and finally accepted her invitation to come out to her house and try her for mediumship. For Florence was never satisfied to be a really fine psychometrist–she wanted to develop deep trance as well. On one particular occasion in 1952 I went to New Jersey armed not only with a high-speed camera and fast black-and-white film, but also a highly treasured wooden box. This box, given to us by a physician friend, contained a piece of medical X-ray film, properly shielded from any and all light or other radiation. Thus we could use it with confidence, secure in the knowledge that if anything appeared on the film at all it would not be due to light leaks or other faults of the equipment.

I placed this wooden box containing the film underneath Florence's foot. On her forehead and arms I fastened several small pieces of infrared film encased in heavy black paper. After Florence had gone into a kind of trance we turned on the lights, which had been extinguished, and took off the film. The film, including the big box with the X-ray film, was then sent to a lab for developing. Imagine my surprise when I saw what had shown up on the X-ray negative. She had exposed this film with her foot–certainly a first in photography, psychic or normal. Was this a crude impression of her own self, seated as she was in her wooden chair? Was it someone else's figure? Surely nothing should have shown up on the negative, for it had never been exposed to either light or radiation of any known kind. Or had it? Had not Florence's own body been the source of radiation, allowing her to be a kind of human camera?

Several months after this initial experiment I returned to Florence's house. In the meantime, her son had died and what had appeared to be a suicide due to asphyxiation in a gas stove, was now open to question. The anguished mother, quite naturally, could not accept the suicide verdict. But there were others in the community who also expressed doubts about the whole matter. The boy had been involved in strange business dealings with men not of the highest caliber, and the possibility of foul play was not entirely impossible. Still, there was no proof, so the case was not being re-opened much as Florence wanted it.

Another time when I visited Florence I came in the company of two friends, Mr. and Mrs. Ben Paratore. Mr. Paratore brought a 35mm Leica and infrared film, and I brought some black bulbs to be used in conjunction with the experiment. Paratore, an aircraft manufacturing executive, was a skeptic, though willing to observe.

Date:

1952.

Place:

Florence Sternfels' residence in Edgewater, New Jersey.

Light conditions:

Total darkness.

Camera:

No camera.

Film:

Medical X-ray in heavy wooden box.

Exposure:

About an hour.

Operator:

Florence Sternfels.

Developing:

Medical lab in area.

Printing:

United Camera shops, New York.

Photo 37 Medical X-ray picture taken with Florence Sternfels' foot, shows figure in chair. No camera was used.

We put out the lights and almost total darkness enveloped the medium, who was seated across the room from us, with a table between us on which freshly cut flowers had been placed. The reason for the flowers was not politeness or a sense of romance, but it is one of the beliefs of spiritualists that freshly cut flowers exude a life force that can be used to manufacture ectoplasm, so necessary in psychic photography.

Again, we tied some shielded infrared film to Florence's forehead and arms, while Mr. Paratore got his camera and flashgun ready. As soon as Florence was apparently in deep trance, I asked him to take pictures at regular intervals. I had also brought a metal trumpet with me which I had made myself the previous day. I placed the trumpet which was made of completely smooth, virgin aluminum, next to the medium. After an hour of deep trance, during which mumbling by the medium was the only discernible noise, we gently woke her and turned the lights on again. Immediately I felt the trumpet and found it hot. Now the trumpet had been far enough from Florence to exclude any possibility of her touching it without getting out of her chair, and she did not move, for I was close enough to her to observe her every movement.

In addition to being inexplicably hot, the metal was now covered by several dozen crudely drawn pictures of sorts, one of which seemed to show a man with his head in an oven, and a small dog near him trying to pull him out. Now it so happens that that is precisely what had taken place when Mrs. Sternfels' son had died. His small cocker spaniel had found the master with his head in the oven, and tried to pull him out. The dog was unable to do so, and had died with him. The metal trumpet was requested by Florence at the time, and I could not very well refuse the distraught mother what was to her the only sign of life from her late boy. I have never been able to get it back, and Florence herself has since passed away.

When the pictures taken by Mr. Paratore in my presence were developed, we discovered to our surprise that a materialization had taken place on Florence's lap. Rising from what is generally called the solar plexus, or the stomach regions where the seat of ectoplasm is said to be, we found at first a white substance forming. Gradually it took on shape and eventually wound up in the form of a small dog's head, with only one ear formed. Noteworthy, too, is the connecting "rod" or link between the flowers and Florence's body. Florence had nothing resting on her lap, nor was there any white object on the table before her that could have been mistaken for the ectoplasm.

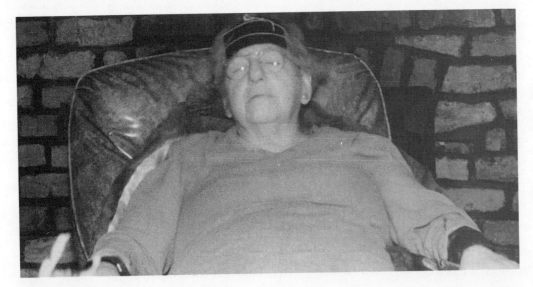

Photo 38

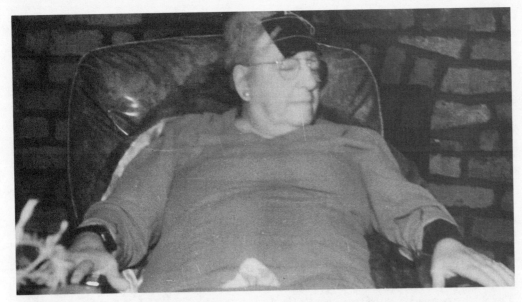

Photo 39

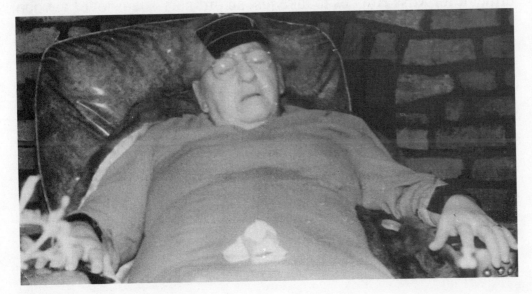

Photo 40

Date:

1952.

Place:

Florence Sternfels' residence, Edgewater, New Jersey.

Light conditions:

Total darkness, black flashbulbs.

Camera:

Leica, 35mm.

Film:

Infrared film. Fresh stock.

Exposure:

Synchronized flash exposure, about 1/25 to 1/50 second.

Operator:

Ben Paratore.

Developing and printing:

Local photography shop.

Photo 38 Florence Sternfels in trance attempting to clarify son's death. No ectoplasm visible as yet.

Photo 39 Ectoplasm starts forming in solar plexus area.

Photo 40 Fully formed ectoplasm shows small dog's head with one ear only formed. Pictures taken with infrared flash.

79

XIV
THE PSYCHIC PHOTOGRAPHY
OF MARIE HUGHES
AND GERRI WARNER

Marie Hughes spent many years as an executive secretary in business offices. She eventually retired and did the things she had always wanted to do. Among them was the pursuit of a rare gift she knew she had–the psychic ability to take pictures of what was not visible to the naked eye.

Miss Hughes' photographs would show ectoplastic material, sometimes resembling figures, but most often just swirling energy. This happened so often, both indoors and outdoors, that it became difficult for Miss Hughes to take just an ordinary snapshot of anyone or anything!

Two of her pictures, which were taken during a circle session with the great trance medium, the late Ethel Johnson Meyers, and two sitters appear here. Notice the face-like structure superimposed in photos 41 and 42, and what appears to be ectoplastic formations in photo 42.

Obviously, the physical person of Marie Hughes makes this possible, just as it did with the late John Myers, and a handful of other photography mediums.

Date:

May 16, 1979, 9 P.M.

Place:

New York City.

Light conditions:

Indoor electric lighting.

Camera:

Zeiss.

Film:

Kodak color 126.

Exposure:

1/25 second.

Operator:

Marie Hughes.

Photos 41 and 42

Psychic emanations in photographis of medium Ethel Johnson Myers and sitters.

Evidently, Marie Hughes' psychic pyhotography talent was not bound to any particular location. When she was vacationing with friends at Bailing Spring Lakes, Southport, North Carolina, during the July 4th weekend in 1970, a set of pictures was taken of her by her own camera, set on automatic.

The picture here reproduced clearly shows a whitish shape on the right, beginning to form.

HOW THIS PICTURE WAS OBTAINED

Date:

July 3–4th, 1970.

Place:

Southport, North Carolina.

Light:

Normal sunny afternoon.

Camera:

Ansco Speedex 4.5.

Film:

Kodacolor X 80 (120).

Exposure:

1/50 at F: 5.6.

Operator:

Marie Hughes.

Photo 43 Marie Hughes with psychic examination.

Like Hughes, "natural" psychic photography medium, Gerri Warner also possessed the unusual gift of photographing what was not visible to the naked eye. I first heard of Warner through Ethel Johnson Meyers, who brought Miss Warner to my office for a test sitting. This was on November 11, 1976, and Miss Warner used an ordinary Polaroid camera and fast color film to take a number of photographs at random.

Several of these photos are shown here. None of the formations were visible to the naked eye, but Ethel did feel spirit precences in my office when Miss Wagner took the pictures.

After the initial test, I visited Miss Warner in her home in Westchester County, New York, with Meyers. At that time more interesting Polaroid photos were taken.

Photo 44 shows Holzer in his office, with psychic emanations almost obscuring him and the file cabinet.

Photo 45 continues the trend but now the ectoplasm is beginning to take on specific forms. The figure of a man seems to be emerging on the left.

Photo 46 taken of Catherine Holzer shows strong ecto-plasmic material almost enveloping her.

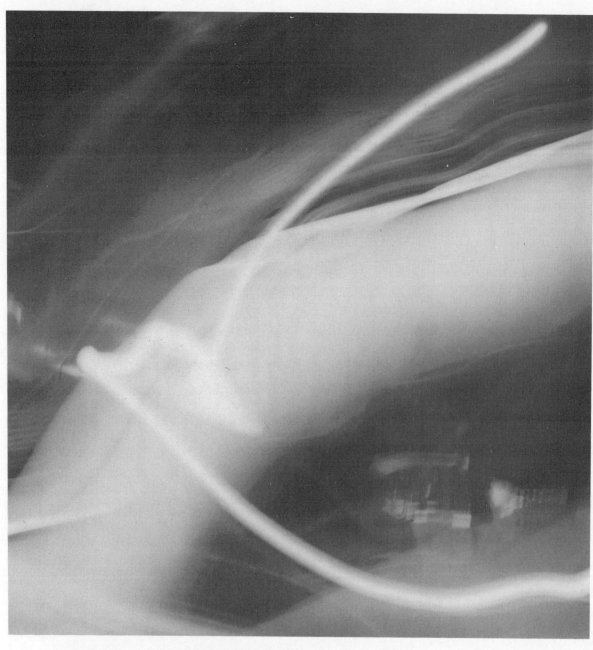

Photos 47 and 48 clearly show the beginning of materialization of what appears to be a female figure.

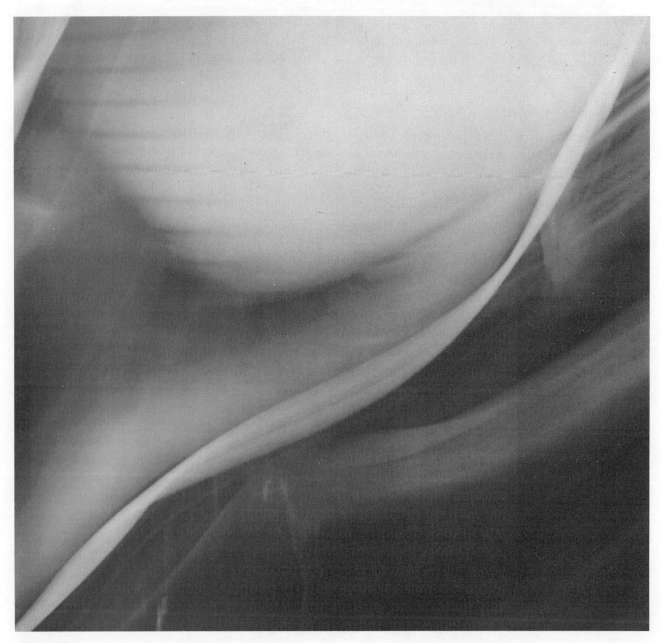

Photo 48

Photo 49 taken of Miss Warner, only shows the lady seated on Holzer's office couch.

PART
TWO

XV
PHOTOGRAPHING THE
RESTLESS ONES:
AUTHENTIC GHOST PICTURES

I think ever since ghosts were talked about in modern times the skeptics must have commented, "Yes, but try and photograph one! Seeing is believing. Anything I can touch, see, hear or smell I'll believe." It would be convenient to agree with this pat philosophy, were it not so patently inadequate. You don't touch, see, hear or smell radio waves, for instance, and yet they are very real and their results can be measured and observed. Mental activity can never be proven objectively to an outsider, as it goes on within the closed confines of man's head. But the consequences of this activity can be observed. Nobody disbelieves thoughts. And yet, sometimes a different yardstick is being used to deal with psychic phenomena. The medium psychically observing an apparition and reporting it in minute detail to the non-psychics concerned with it is exactly as factual as the skeptic having a thought of any kind. Only the environment of our basically materialistic age has taught the skeptic to arbitrarily reject certain mental impressions because they do not conform to the image of the world he or she has been brought up in. The will to disbelieve regardless of evidence, so long as the evidence is contrary to *accepted* belief, is the strongest and most widespread of all human motivations, even stronger than the will to *believe*.

Despite my firm conviction that ghosts were indeed real in the same sense as radio waves, being made up of electric impulses put together in unique forms called human personalities, I looked for a way to prove this conviction to the outside world. Evidence excluding information obtained by my mediums by ordinary means was piling up, and my books are full of the details. But the Chinese proverb reminds us that one picture is worth more than ten thousand words.

There is a basic difference between a psychic photograph which tends to implement communication between two states of being and is usually the result of experimental desire on the part of a group of people to get results, and the entirely spontaneous, unexpected, unintended photograph of a ghost in his or her haunted habitat. Ghost photographs have been published almost since the beginning of photography itself. As with psychic pictures, I can neither affirm or assail their authenticity, for I was not present when they were taken. But in 1937 a photograph was taken under conditions no fair-minded scientist could criticize. The setting was Raynham Hall, Norfolk, England, the ancestral seat of the Marquess Townshend.

Three-hundred-year-old Raynham Hall is a rambling structure of some size within a 20,000-acre estate, where American servicemen were stationed during World War II. Since then the house has been closed to outsiders and, since the Townshends are not exactly afflicted with poverty, the widely practiced custom of admitting tourists for half a crown never invaded the august portals of the Hall.

As reported in the January 4, 1937, issue of *Life* magazine, it all started innocently enough with an order to photograph the interior of the stately mansion. Indre Shira, Ltd., a London firm of Court photographers was hired to perform the task. In September 1936 the company sent Captain Hubert C. Provand and an assistant to Raynham Hall to do the job.

Immediately after his arrival, Captain Provand set out to work. He had no use for the supernatural, and if he had heard of the ghostly legends he put no stock in them. But one of his cameras was smashed by seemingly unseen hands. Still he refused to accept the possibility of a ghost being the culprit. At one point during their meticulous work of photographing the interior of the Hall, the two men found themselves facing the famous grand staircase in the Great Hall downstairs. "Look!" the assistant suddenly said, and pointed toward the staircase, terror etched on his face. The captain looked but saw nothing. The young man insisted he saw a white figure slowly descending the stairs. "Well," the skeptical captain replied, "if you're so sure of it, let's photograph it." Quickly they pointed their camera toward the staircase and made an exposure. This was done with flash, but one must remember that in 1936 flash photography was not what it is today, and the intensity of the flash light very much weaker than with modern flashbulbs. At this the figure dissolved–at least the assistant reported it was no longer visible to him. The two photographers then sealed the plate and took it to the chemists' firm of Blake, Sanford & Blake, where the negative was developed. The chemists attested to the fact that nothing had been wrong with either negative or developing, and that the figure on the staircase was not due to slipshod handling of any kind.

HOW THIS PICTURE WAS OBTAINED

Date:

September 1936.

Place:

Raynham Hall, Norfolk, England.

Light conditions:

Daytime, flashlight.

Camera:

Still camera, 8 x 10.

Exposure:

Flash.

Operator:

Captain Provand of Indre Shira, Ltd.

Developing:

Blake, Sandford, & Blake.

Photo 50 The world famous ghost photo of Rayham Hall.

The striking figure is that of a woman in flowing dress, descending the staircase. It is white and smokelike, and the stairs can be seen through it. When the results were shown to the Townshends, there was a moment of embarrassed silence. Then the photograph was compared with a portrait of Lady Dorothy Walpole which hung in one of the upstairs passages. It was also pretty much the same as the reported apparition of the lady seen by a number of Townshend house guests over the years.

What made Dorothy Walpole a ghost, way back in the 1780s, was a little inconvenience called mental depressions, but in those days this was considered a disease not fit to be discussed in polite society. Being of gentle birth, the lady was therefore "contained" in a room upstairs and spent her last years in it, finally passing across the threshold of death no longer in her right mind. Perhaps she was not aware of this change and considers Raynham Hall still her rightful home, and herself free now to range it at will, and to smash intruding photographers' cameras if she so desires.

Life published the picture with all the facts and left it to the readers to make up their own minds. I have shown this picture on national television and before many college audiences and have never failed to get gasps from the audience, for it is indeed the very model of what a ghost picture should look like.

It occurred to me that there should be a reasonably controlled way of obtaining photographs of so-called ghosts, by simply photographing as many haunted places as possible under varying conditions and from many angles. If ghosts are two-dimensional in character, as I suspected, then hitting the proper angle or plane of their existence would be extremely hazardous, and the chance of finding it not very great. On the other hand, I had nothing to lose by trying.

Impressed by the Raynham ghost picture (known as "the Brown Lady of Raynham Hall"), I discussed this subject with Eileen Garrett, president of Parapsychology Foundation. The foundation had in the past sponsored me, giving me modest grants to carry on my work of investigating haunted houses and mediums. But at the time Mrs. Garrett had no use for the subject of psychic photography, assuring me that to the best of her knowledge it was all fraudulent and not worth the effort.

I found myself disagreeing with my old friend, and went on my own with the research. My camera was to be a handmade Zeiss, Super Ikonta B model, which is exceptionally well suited for work in dark areas, as its large lens has a high degree of light sensitivity and its mechanical parts are precision-made. Above all, this camera has a lock that prevents accidental double exposure. In order to advance the film, the key has to be turned a full 180 degrees. Only then does the mechanism snap into place. An imperfect turn will not activate the camera. This is important, as it means that only square pictures of the exact size the camera was built for can be exposed by it under normal conditions. No odd sizes, oblong pictures or other accidents of size and shape are possible. When the key has been properly turned, one must first cock the shutter fully and hear it click into place. Only then is the camera ready for work. By depressing the exposure button on top of the camera, the cocked shutter is released and the picture is taken. In order to take a second picture, the entire process has to be repeated. If one of the three steps is omitted, the camera will not work, and double exposures cannot occur. In fact, the only way to get double exposure with this camera is to take the film out and replace it in the camera–in other words, out-and-out fraud.

Next I decided that only the fastest film would do, since any form of flashlight or strong artificial light would destroy the sensitive psychic elements I set out to photograph. Besides, one might be accused of light reflections or refractions. I therefore decided to work only with soft light; that is, daylight or ordinary room light. The only film fast enough to give me acceptable results with so little light was the Agfa Record Isopan, a black-and-white film with very little grain that can be developed to a 1200 ASA rating, about 12 times higher than that of the average black-and-white film used by amateurs. Unfortunately when I started this experiment in 1964, there was no really fast color film. Things have improved since, but not nearly enough to allow me to substitute color film on all occasions.

Now I did not deliberately set out to photograph a ghost. I never thought that would work, nor do I now think so. I took large amounts of location pictures, with as much variety of angle and timing as possible. If ghosts are electromagnetic fields impressed on the atmosphere of their demise, then they should be capable of being measured by sensitive instruments. They have been measured by Geiger counters on a number of occasions. But I wanted something visual also, and it occurred to me that psychic sensitivity was somehow related to magnetism. Could not film also record these impressions? This was pure guesswork on my part until April 1964. Then something happened that showed me I was on the right track with this quest.

One of my longest and most difficult investigations concerned a pleasant-looking bungalow in Los Angeles, built arount 1929. After a couple of years in the house, its owners were forced to sublease because of financial reverses, and for nine years strangers lived in the house, not all of whom could be recalled by the owners. It was during that period of estrangement from their house that something evidently took place to leave an indelible imprint on its atmosphere. When they repossessed their home, the L.'s soon discovered that they were being plagued by a variety of psychic phenomena that frightened them. At the same time they started to make inquiries into the events that had taken place at the house in their absence.

The disturbances ranged from measured footsteps where no one was seen to walk, to raps at their door, and from the feelings of presences–there were actually two, one male and one female–to such specific and detailed occurrences as a fight to the finish taking place audibly, but not visually, in the living room over and over again, only to stop abruptly when a member of the family opened the door from one of the bedrooms. The center of ghostly manifestations seemed to have been the bedroom where Helen L., the owner's oldest daughter, slept, and the patio in the back of the house. On one occasion the noise of a struggle on the furniture-filled patio awoke all members of the family, which consisted of Helen L., her aged mother and another sister. But on checking this out they found the furniture completely untouched. It was then that they remembered a call from their erstwhile neighbors, while the L.'s were living elsewhere, advising them that a terrible fight had taken place in their house. The neighbors had clearly heard the noise of furniture being broken. When the L.'s repossessed their house they found that the report had not been exaggerated. Broken furniture filled their house. Several witnesses confirmed hearing footsteps of someone they did not see, and Helen L. heard the sounds of someone trying to break into her bedroom through the French doors from the patio. That someone was a young girl, judging from the sound of the footsteps. The other footsteps, heard also by a number of witnesses, were heavy footfalls of a man in pursuit. In addition, the sounds of a wild party resounded in the darkness around her, and on one occasion she heard a voice telling her to get out of her own house. Naturally, Helen L. was upset at all this and asked for my help. On my first visit I made sure that she was a reasonably rational individual. I later returned in the company of the head of the Los Angeles chapter of the American Society for Psychic Research, as witness. I was also accompanied by Maxine Bell, a local psychic. Without any foreknowledge of where she was being taken by me, or an opportunity to talk to the owners of the house, Mrs.Bell clairvoyantly described the sudden violence that had erupted in this house in 1948, involving two men and a girl.

With the head of the Los Angeles chapter of the American Society for Psychic Research had come an associate, an engineer by profession, who also had psychic leanings. Separately from Mrs Bell, he described his impressions of an older man and a very young girl, a teenager, who had died at the same time here. As I always do, I took routine location pictures all over the house with black-and-white fast film and without artificial light sources. I was quite alone in the haunted bedroom when I took six or seven exposures.

When these were later developed by the laboratory employed by Fotoshop of New York, one of them also showed a young girl in what appears to be a negligé standing at the window, looking toward the bed. The figure is solid enough, although the left flank is somewhat illuminated by the infiltrating sunshine from the patio. But on close inspection it is clear that the figure is not actually standing on the floor near the French doors, but rather *above* the floor near the bed. I examined the room again later to make sure no curtains could have been mistaken for this apparition; there were no curtains. Since the picture was taken, I made several trips back to Los Angeles to help send the two ghosts away, and much additional evidence has piled up. But essentially it was the story of a young girl with men fighting over her. Someone seemed to have been hurt in the process. There were indications that a body might still be hidden in the garden, but to this date the owner of the house has refused to dig for it. After the L.'s had moved back into their house, they had found blood spots on the floor.

I was very much shaken up by this picture, especially as it came quite unexpectedly. None of the other exposures on the same roll showed anything significant. I felt that the presence of both Mrs. Bell and Helen L. in the immediate vicinity was responsible for the picture, as I never considered myself psychic. I should add that I have since gone back to the same house several times, and never been able to duplicate the ghost picture. This is not surprising in view of my conviction that such apparitions are two-dimensional, and there are countless planes possible within the same 360-degree area. It is perhaps a moot question whether we are dealing here with ghosts in the strict sense of the term, meaning a human personality "hung up" in time and outside space, or with a mere impression, an imprint of violence left behind by an event in the past. Either way, it is a paranormal occurrence in the sense of parapsychology, but I am inclined to consider this particular case one of a genuine ghost, inasmuch as the personality did react in various ways at various times and in general showed traits of a disturbed human personality, something a "dead" imprint just would not do.

Date:

April 18, 1964, 3 P.M.

Place:

Ardmore Boulevard, Los Angeles (exact location withheld), the house of Helen L.. Photo 2 was taken on garden patio, where presumably murder took place

Light conditions:

Normally bright afternoon, sunny. Inside the house, windows open. The bedroom windows, actually French doors, are covered only by a pair of blinds. Sunlight from the garden and patio coming through French doors. No reflecting surfaces inside room, except a mirror completely outside field of vision. Bedspread opaque, carpet opaque, no artificial light.

Camera:

Super Ikonata B, Zeiss, in excellent working condition.

Film:

Agfa Record Isopan 120, fast black-and-white film, rated 1200 ASA.

Exposure:

Two seconds from a firm support, camera resting on linen chest in back of bedroom. Normally, at this exposure, film should be burned completely and no image should show.

Operator:

Hans Holzer, alone in bedroom; medium Maxine Bell and owner of house, Helen L., seated outside bedroom in adjacent living room.

Photo 51 The Ardmore Boulevard ghost girl.

Photo 52 The Ardmore Boulevard ghost girl.

100

XVI
GHOSTLY "PRESENCES"
CAUSING VISUAL
PHENOMENA

Ghosts want to reach out in any way they can to make their continued presence in the place known to observers. They create, by their energies, psychic fields which can sometimes be photographed.

Not every manifestation of psychic fields in haunted or otherwise phsychically active areas leads to full apparitions. Sometimes the energies present are not strong enough to manifest an entire personality, or the phenomenon belongs to that shadowy category of psychic impressions left behind by a traumatic event in the past, without the continuing presence of an actual personality. I have found on many occasions that such fields do exist and that they can be photographed.

No long ago *Life* magazine published photographs of rooms taken some time after people had left them. Yet the photographs showed the figures of these persons as if they were still present. The impressions are shallow and not sharp, but they are undoubtedly those of people. *Life*'s photographs were produced through heat-sensitive cameras, not psychically. But there is a relationship between the heat imprint and the psychic imprint, inasmuch as both are energy patterns impressed on the atmosphere of an area.

I never searched for the electromagnetic fields I feel are present in the areas of emotional turmoil in a house or other enclosure, since I could not very well pinpoint them, dealing as I was with two-dimensional matters in a three-dimensional area. But by pointing my camera in as many directions as possible I greatly increased the possibility of accidentally hitting the right plane. Theoretically, I could take an unlimited number of pictures in such a room, moving my camera angle ever so slightly, and then I would certainly have to include the haunted area. But practically speaking, this is a monumental task.

The following pages present some extraordinary takes, all of my authorship, all with the same camera and type of film. What these pictures have in comon are "multiple exposure" type areas that are not multiple exposures. In every case, double exposure was impossible, film was fresh and unspoiled, developing and printing the work of experts, and the Zeiss camera had been checked within a year for possible light leaks and damage. Nothing was found.

Photo 53 was taken at St. Mark's-in-the-Bowerie Church in New York City. It was number two on a roll of 11 exposures. None of the other nine exposures shows anything unusual; all were pictures of the church interior. But this photo clearly shows multiple exposure patterns. The effect seems to be similar to a picture taken with a large mirror present in the area, to reflect part of the room. There was no such mirror in the church when I took the pictures. But it may well be that the psychically active area *acted* like a mirror to create the unusual distortions seen here. Although most of the details of the picture are seen twice, there appear in the upper third, center, a white dot and line not duplicated nearby or elsewhere in the photograph. They look like ectoplasm rods. The picture was taken in the heart of the haunted area, near a pew where a ghost had been observed.

Photos 54 and 55 show a series of pictures taken during a seance in June Havoc's old townhouse in New York. Sybil Leek was the medium, and she is seen in the picture standing in the back of the downstairs living room, which was the center of poltergeist activities. I have told the story of this remarkable haunting in *Yankee Ghosts,* including the trance session in which a ghostly presence spoke through Mrs. Leek, identifying herself under my prodding as one Lucy Ryan, a camp follower in the year 1792, whose soldier served in a regiment commanded by a certain Napier. The next day I was able to identify the commander as Col. George Napier and confirm much of the wraith's story. While we were preparing for the trance portion of our investigation, Mrs. Leek stood idly by, admiring Miss Havoc's furniture and bric-a-brac. It was at this point that I started to take photos from the area of the "outer" half of the

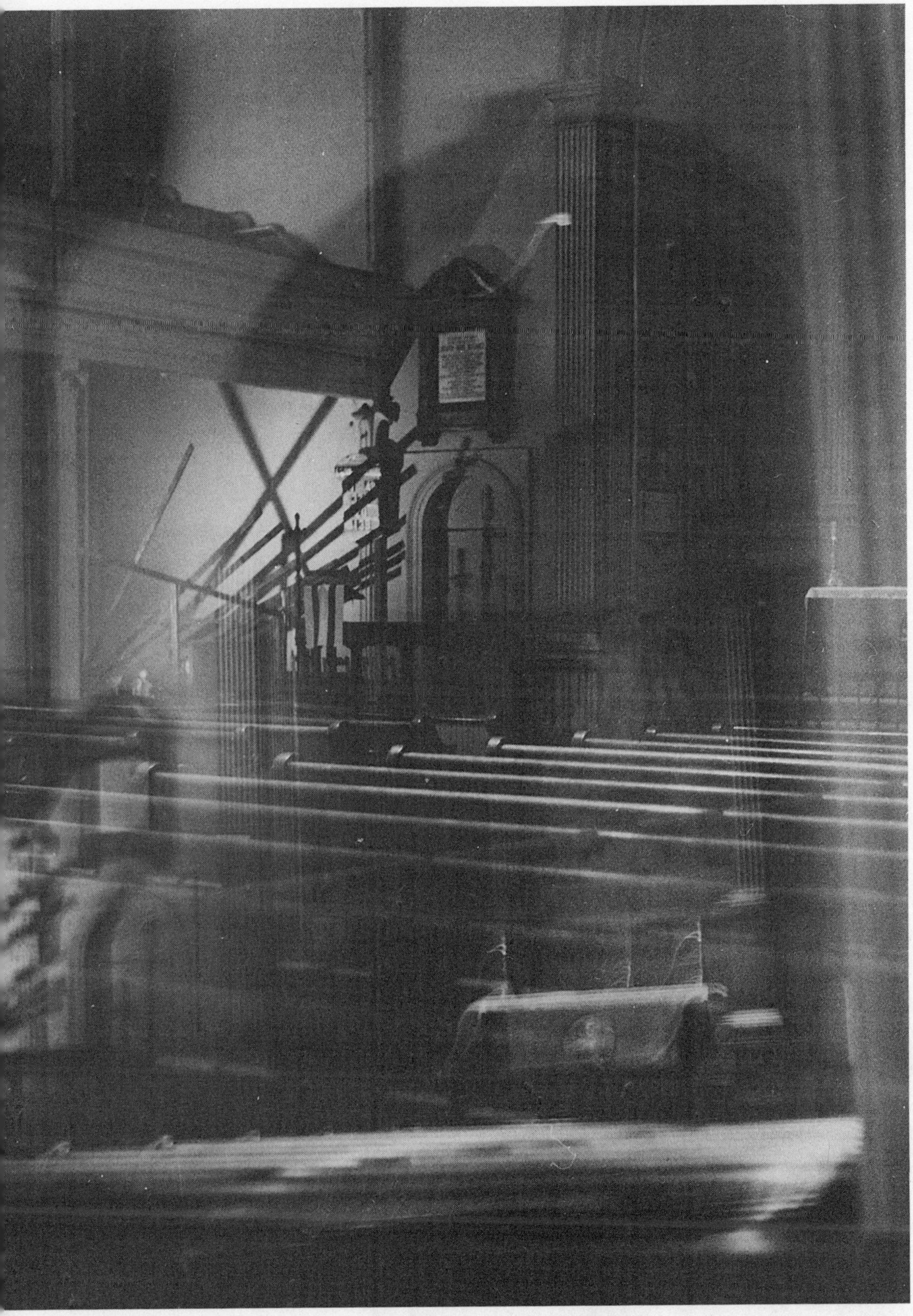

Photo 53 *Haunted St. Marks-in-the-Bowerie, New York City.*

HOW THIS PICTURE WAS OBTAINED

Date:

March 15, 1960. Afternoon.

Place:

St. Mark's-in-the-Bowerie Church, New York City.

Light conditions:

Available daylight, pretty dim.

Camera:

Super Ikonta B, 120.

Film:

Agfa Record Isopan, 120.

Exposure:

Two seconds, on firm surface.

Operator:

Hans Holzer; also present, mediumistic Mary M.

Developing and printing:

United Camera, New York.

large living room, pointing my Zeiss camera toward the right rear, where most of the disturbances had taken place.

In photo 54, you can see the floorboards as plain, roughly hewn Victorian wood; the wall to the right is covered with bric-a-brac and there is no obstruction whatever between viewer and wall. Photo 55 was taken about 10 minutes later, after we had all sat down. My former wife, Catherine, is seen on the left. The floorboards now look transparent, although there was and is no way in which they could be made to reflect in this manner. Furthermore, the wall on the right is now blocked from full view by a black, irregular shape. Nothing within the camera bellows could account for this obstruction, nor can film or print be blamed for the sudden appearance of this black area.

Ten minutes later, another exposure was made after Leek had gotten up again and stood on the exact spot where I had earlier (before her arrival) heard the poltergeist noises myself. This time the arrangement of the room shows a marked change. To begin with, my ex-wife's knees seem cut off by a spreading reflection of the floor, as if ice or a mirror were covering the wooden boards. If this were a true, optical reflection, however, everything would have to appear *in proportion*. But this is not the case with this phenomenon. The back of the chair behind my ex-wife does "reflect" in the floor surface, yet her knees, so much closer to the floor, do not show at all. The figure of Leek appears strangely foreshortened. A streak of light, not accounted for by any form of leakage from the tightly packed roll of film, appears bottom right. And the black amorphous shape has now changed contours considerably.

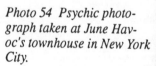

Photo 54 Psychic photograph taken at June Havoc's townhouse in New York City.

Photo 55 *Sybil Leek and pyschic phenomenon*

HOW THESE PICTURES
WERE OBTAINED

Date:

October, 1964. Evening.

Place:

June Havoc's townhouse,
New York City.

Light conditions:

Very bright electric room
lights, no flash.

Camera:

Zeiss Super Ikonta B, 120.

Film:

Agfa Record Isopan, 120.

Exposure:

1/25 second at F/2.8.

Operator:

Hans Holzer.

Developing and printing:

Fotoshop, New York.

Photo 56 *Sybil Leek in June Havoc's haunted house.*

XVII
THE "1780 HOUSE"
GHOSTS

One of the most curious of all pictures I have ever taken with my camera also involved the kind of back-up proof very few psychic investigations get. The story itself concerns a house in North Stamford, Connecticut, then owned by Bob and Dotty Cowan, rational and intelligent individuals who make their living as art director and actress respectively. They had been living for some time in a colonial house dating back to 1780 (so they were told), but lately the uncanny noises, footsteps and other strange goings-on had been such that they decided to call for help, and I was brought in.

In mid February 1964, I visited the house with my ex-wife, Catherine. The story of the psychic phenomena in the house and my two visits culminating in an exorcism was reported in my book, *Ghosts I've Met*. During our first visit to the house, we were standing in a room on the main floor of the building when I clearly heard heavy footfalls overhead. Catherine heard them, too, and so did the Cowans, who managed a wan, triumphant "I told you so" type of smile.

I raced up the wooden stairs to the upper floor only to find myself in the dark, literally, for the upper floor was empty and none of the lights were on. Nobody had been walking on that floor; that is, nobody of flesh and blood. Next to the room in which I had heard the ghostly footsteps was a smaller room partitioned off from the larger room but most likely once part of the same living quarters. It was in this room that Mrs. Cowan had had a most unusual visual experience not long before. "Like lightning," she described it, "a bright light suddenly come and gone.

Now, I accept the power of suggestion, since I myself am a professional hypnotist and know all the tricks of the trade. Consequently I took very good care that the reported experience by Mrs. Cowan did not intrude on my subconscious mind. I sat there in the dark room, definitely hostile toward any similar manifestation rather than eager for it to happen to me.

Before the lights had been turned off I had made a careful search of the room and its appointments. The windows were placed in such a manner as to make any reflection of passing headlights out of the question. There was no road immediately near the house, only the dark countryside surrounding the building. I tried the stairwell lights to see if they would reflect into the room, but all they did was cast a small amount of low-intensity light into the area nearest to the door of the room.

The four of us then turned out the lights and sat down quietly, waiting for such phenomena as might honor us. A few minutes went by and the only noise we heard was the ticking of a grandfather clock. At this precise moment my eyes were fastened on the back wall of the little room. Suddenly I noticed a flash of white light in the corner opposite me. It was a bright flash, as if a photographic flashgun had just gone off. The whole phenomenon took only a moment, but Dotty Cowan also saw it and excitedly exclaimed, "There it is again–exactly as I saw it!"

After this initial experience I returned to the house with the late medium Ethel Johnson Meyers, without telling her anything about the case or our own experiences. During the first visit she managed to contact one of the entities in the house, and the rest on a second visit in December. Between the two visits the activities at the house increased considerably. Footsteps were heard and lights were clearly seen in the empty house by the Cowans as the approached in the evening. They heard noises not easily explained on ordinary grounds.

The gist of the two seances was a harrowing story of crime and guilt. A young girl named Lucy or Laurie was born in 1756. Her grandfather, Samuel, disapproved of a certain young man's paying attention to his grandaughter. The young man's name was Benjamin. Samuel confessed to having killed Benjamin and thrown his body down a well in 1774. A family name was also mentioned, which I took to be Harmon, although I could not hear it too clearly. Apparently the body was later taken from the well and both grandfather Samuel and young Benjamin were buried on the hill "in back of a white structure on these grounds." Moreover, the entranced medium reported, both tombstones had been mishandled by vandals and were broken off close to the earth. At the time I wrote my report on this case, the house was known on record back to 1780 only, hence the name. But I said almost prophetically then—"Could not another building have occupied the area?" That was in the spring of 1965.

On November 1, 1965, the *Stamford Advocate* carried an interesting story. The Stamford Historical Society had been doing some exploring in a house next to the 1780 house. Accidentally they came across an old well on a hill. The owners of the adjacent house had been digging up old stones, one of which turned out to be a gravestone. With the help of the historical society volunteers, they managed to find five more fragments of gravestones. When properly cleaned, the stones turned out to be "broken off at the ground" indeed, inscribed BENJAMIN, SAMUEL and BARNUM. Also, one fragment with the date "1746" proving that the 1780 house was older than 1780, since this was once all one and the same property. Physical proof for psychic information is not always obtained in so spectacular a manner, but in this case the jigsaw puzzle did indeed fall into place.

During my third visit, Ethel Johnson Meyers and I "sat" in the "ship" room in front. The trance took place in that part of the house. At one point I felt compelled to take some photographs in the existing electric room light. I aimed my camera toward a chair in which my ex-wife Catherine was sitting. I briefly exposed the film, for the room was pretty well lit. Imagine my surprise when the roll was developed. To begin with, the "odd picture" on this roll—the only one with unusual characteristics—was one and a half times larger than all others, something quite incomprehensible in the case of my Zeiss camera. Ordinarily only square pictures can be taken with it.

Secondly, a writing desk which stood *in back of* me showed up on the negative where it could only have appeared if I had used a special mirror. There was no such mirror.

Finally, there is a large burst of white light in the center of the picture, a burst of light very similar to what we had observed upstairs a little earlier!

*Photo 57 Stamford, Connecticut, haunted house is site of re-
markable picture, showing writing desk on left, which actually was behind camera, and white energy burst to left of
Mrs. Holzer.*

Date:

December 15, 1964. Evening.

Place:

Cowan house, Stamford, Connecticut.

Light conditions:

Strong room light.

Camera:

Super Ikonta B, 120.

Film:

Agfa Record Isopan, 120.

Exposure:

2.8 lens and 1/25 second.

Operator:

Hans Holzer.

Developing and printing:

Fotoshop, New York City.

XVIII
THE ASTORIA GHOST

Astoria, Long Island, is a very ordinary part of New York City. Ghosts are the furthest thing from people's minds in Astoria. But the ghosts either don't know that, or don't care.

The late Betty Ritter, one of the best photography mediums and psychic readers, introduced me to the extraordinary photographs taken of her stepmother, Catherine Vecchio, of Astoria.

It seems Mrs. Vecchio, who was psychic also, sat for a "portrait" by Betty Ritter. A box camera and black-and-white film were used. With two powerful psychic sources and their energies present, it is no surprise that something unusual would occur.

Evidently, an elderly European gentleman who once resided in the very house the photos were taken could not resist the opportunity to manifest. Clearly, he was restless and unable to proceed into the next stage of existence, or perhaps only lonely for contact with our world. Be this as it may, the portrait of the old gentleman all but replaced the face of Mrs. Vecchio.

**HOW THIS PICTURE
WAS OBTAINED**

Date:

November 28, 1965.

Place:

Astoria, Long Island.

Light conditions:

Daylight.

Camera: Kodak box camera.

Film:

Standard black-and-white Kodak.

Operator:

Betty Ritter.

Developing:

Betty Ritter.

Photo 58 and 59 The Astoria Ghost manefestation

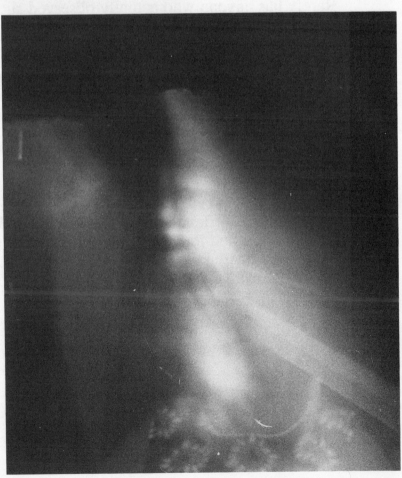

XIX
A GHOSTLY
APPARITION IN
THE SKY

Reports of miraculous apparitions of the Virgin Mary, even of Jesus, and of various angels and saints, come to public attention from time to time. Invariably, the believers immediately flock to such sites mainly to obtain miraculous cures, or at least be spiritually enriched.

Since ancient times, people have reported these events, usually interpreting them as the spirit visitations of heavenly personalities. Rarely has anyone who actually observed such an apparition considered the visions to be spiritual beings of lesser stature, such as relatives or friends of worshippers, or simply people who have passed on to the next stage of existence, and for one or the other reason, decided to manifest in this manner and place.

An interesting and unsought photograph was taken by Cecilia Hood, a very spiritual lady from upstate New York. Rev. Hood is an ordained spiritual minister and has practiced as such for many years. On October 14, 1975, she shared with me an extraordinary original photograph which falls into this category. The picture was actually taken in 1971 during a terrible storm in rural Pennsylvania by Rev. Hood's friend and associate Margie Brooks. There was a terrible flood and the sky was very dark. Suddenly Miss Brooks observed a figure in white in the sky and took this picture. Was it a way those from the other side wanted to reassure her of her safety?

Photo: 60 The figure in the clouds appearing in Pennsylvania photograph.

HOW THIS PICTURE
WAS OBTAINED

Date:

1971, during the big Pennsylvania flood.

Place:

Rural Pennsylvania.

Light conditions:

Dark storm cloud, daytime.

Camera:

Black-and-white amateur camera.

Operator:

Margie Brooks.

XX
THE GHOSTLY
TELEVISION PICTURE

I have spent much time investigating a Victorian manor house called The Cedars, in Rye, New York, belonging to Mr. and Mrs. John Smythe. Mrs. Smythe was better known as Molly Guion, the celebrated portrait painter. The house is a sprawling, mid-19th century manor house standing on a bluff overlooking the New Haven Railroad. It was built around 1860 by Jared B. Peck, and rises to four floors. There is a wide porch around it on the ground level, and the house itself stands under tall trees protecting it from the road and giving the entire estate a feeling of remoteness despite the fact that the grounds are not very large.

Downstairs there is a huge living room, filled with fine antiques tastefully matched to the period the house represents. In addition, there is a sitting room and a kitchen. A ghostly apparition has been seen near the kitchen, as well as on the upper stories.

The second floor contains many smaller rooms. A winding stairway leads to the third floor. Here the rooms are even smaller, since evidently that part of the house was once used as the servants' quarters. There is a sharply angled stairway leading to the attic, closed off by a wooden door. This door has been heard to open and slam shut by itself many times. The attic was Molly Guion's studio. Here she did her work, uninterrupted if possible by both visitors and ghosts.

Photo 61 *The Haunted House in Rye, New York.*

There is also a small bedroom on the attic floor. Mr. Smythe slept in it once and reported footsteps he could not explain on rational grounds.

The phenomena included opening noises of the front door, swinging of the chain when no one was about, and, above all, the movement of heavy objects by their own volition. On one occasion, a carving knife took off in the well-lit kitchen and flung itself at the feet of Mr. and Mrs. Smythe, as if to call attention to someone's presence. On another occasion, an ashtray flew from its place to land slowly on the floor of one of the upstairs bedrooms.

I held a number of seances at The Cedars, both with Ethel Johnson Meyers and with Sybil Leek. As a result of my investigations, I learned that there are present two different entities–perhaps three. The door-slamming ghost may be that of a former owner, who spent her last remaining years shut up in one of the small upstairs bedrooms. Perhaps she was put there by her family and resented her confinement. At any rate, there are markings on the door of one of the small bedrooms on the third floor indicating that a heavy lock must have been in place at one time.

The second entity goes back to the early 18th century and connects with an earlier house standing on the same spot. A fire is said to have consumed that earlier building, and the entity still recalls the horror of being burned.

Finally, there is a young woman who died tragically at the house in this century and whose presence may account for some of the continuing phenomena.

Several years ago, I filed my concluding report about the ghostly goings-on in the beautiful old Victorian "Gingerbread" house. I thought that would be the end of the matter but we never were able to hold a final "rescue circle," as the owners with whom I had worked for so many years, passed on. The house then passed into the hands of Peter Behrendt, a pragmatically minded German-born corporate executive who enjoyed the house with his family and was not in the least disturbed by any ghostly manifestations.

But eventually "PM," a syndicated television program, asked me to present the story and the owners graciously allowed us to do so–still unconcerned about the whole matter. And while Peter Behrendt, the owner, was not prepared to admit he had ghosts in the house, his wife, Barbara, was not so sure. I have no further plans to visit or dislodge the remaining ghosts. But I am concerned about the girl who appeared in one frame of 16mm film the ABC TV crew brought back from the house, and which to this day has left some of the people at ABC in a state of puzzlement.

Instead of showing the house, which the crew was filming, one single frame showed a strange configuration. There is a face on the extreme right of the shot, a male face (the father?) and a female head further to the central portion of what appears to be psychic energy–something frequently occurring in pictures of this kind. But below appears a signature, possibly in mirror script. The name–if that is what it is–starts with the letter S. Incidentally, the name of the girl who died in the fire began with the letter S.

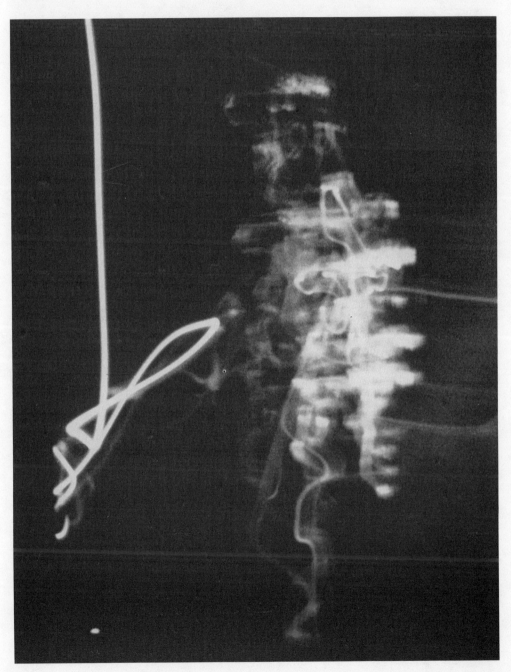

Photo 62 The 16mm film frame showing faces and ectoplasm

HOW THIS PICTURE
WAS OBTAINED

Date:

Winter 1985. Nighttime.

Place:

Rye, New York. 10 Barberry Lane. Outside the house.

Light:

Television floodlights normal for nighttime shooting.

Camera:

16 mm film camera, Arriflex.

Film::

16mm Ectachrome film.

Exposure:

24 frames.

Operator:

ABC TV camera crew.

Development:

ABC lab.

*Photo 63: The unfortu-
nate Lady*

**HOW THIS PICTURE
WAS OBTAINED**

Date:

Winter 1985. Nighttime.

Place:

Rye, New York. 10 Barber-
ry Lane. Outside the house.

Light:

Television floodlights normal for nighttime shooting.

Camera:

16 mm film camera, Arri-
flex.

Film::

16mm Ectachrome film.

Exposure:

24 frames.

Operator:

ABC TV camera crew.

Development:

ABC lab.

L. R. Bronk.   Portchester, N. Y.

XXI
ELLA,
WHO CAN'T
FIND REST

I call spirits who cannot let go of their earthly environment "*stay-behinds*," because they are so used to it and fear the uncertainty of the hearafter. They are ghosts in the sense that wanting to hang on to the physical dimension is not in their best interest, yet they are not irrational as are ghosts who died very tragically or traumatically.

Often, these people know very well they are "dead" but choose to ignore it. Sometimes they get attached to new owners of what was once their home and derive energies from them which, in turn, enable them to manifest stronger. This is particularly true where there are young children in a household.

The case of Ella and her farmhouse in Vineland, New Jersey, is particularly interesting because Ella made "contact" with me in a way she had not done before–through photography. Up until I photographed her, Ella had been a very real, but not very tangible "co-resident" of the house for years.

The owners had called on me to come out and persuade Ella to move on. This was their report.

The Joneses moved into the old farmhouse in the summer of 1975. Tom Jones had been a pilot and captain in the U.S. Air Force when he and Nancy met in her native Little Rock, Arkansas. The Vineland house belonged to Tom Jones' father, and he had promised to restore it to its former glory, if possible. The woods around it had to be cleared with bulldozers so they could do some farming again, every window in the house was broken, screens missing, and filth on every one of the three floors.

Jones left the Air Force and settled down to married life as a supervisor for a large food processing comapny. At first he was going to do most of the restoration work in the house himself, but soon realized he needed professional help. A succession of carpenters and paperhangers were brought in to lend a hand. They rebuilt the third floor, making many structural changes, perhaps inadvertedly setting off something of the uncanny. The day the Joneses moved in, Leslie Anne was 3, little September was six months old, and Thomas Morgan had not been born yet.

"The first time I walked into this house, I felt something horrible had happened in it–but I thought it was my imagination at first," said Nancy Jones. Soon Nancy had forgotten all about her initial apprehension regarding the old house. "About four weeks afterwards, I was alone in the house. I had just put the children to bed–when I heard children *laughing outside*. I was standing in the downstairs dining room at the time, so I ran outside to look. There were no children outside. I ran upstairs and found the kids in bed taking their aftenoon nap."

That summer, Nancy heard the invisible children several times more–always when her own were safely in bed. The Joneses were beginning to wonder about the house. Their discomfort was greatly increased when Nancy discovered Leslie Anne in lively conversation with an unseen "friend." The Joneses were not particularly worried about ghosts. They had always had an open mind about life after death, and it was merely a matter of curiosity to find out if they shared their house with something–or someone–from the past who had not quite left it.

Finally, the Joneses called in their friend, Lois, who had some knowledge of psychic matters. "We decided to hold a little seance in the front parlor," Tom Jones explained. "We were trying to talk out this thing with the unseen children once and for all. But all of a sudden Lois started to talk like the children, conversing with an unknown child in a very high-pitched, childish tone...they were talking about playing *outside*...it was rather entertaining, nothing at all fearful...and after that seance, the phenomenon of the unseen children disappeared...except for the gravestone." I had been listening with silent interest, but now my ears perked up. I had seen the gravestone in back of the house. "We found the gravestone when we cleared the land and had to move it periodically to get it out of

Photo 64 The old farmhouse.

Photo 65 The Joneses

Photo 66 Tombstone of the children.

the way, finally leaving it in the field about a hundred yards away from the house. But after our little seance, all of a sudden it just decided to locate itself right outside our back door," recounted Tom Jones.

The Joneses had tried to find the grave site, but without success. The stone marked the grave of two children, ages 13 and seven weeks who had died in 1891 and 1889 respectively, but had for some unknown reason been placed under the same stone. The children had been part of the family that had built the house in the 19th century.

"Funny thing is, it would have taken four strong men to move that gravestone....and none of us did it. Happened the day after we held that memorial seance," commented Tom. The Joneses figured the children were now at rest, but they soon discovered their house was not. About a year later, Nancy was walking up the stairs to the master bedroom on the second floor, when she saw a tall, slender man standing "over" her bed. "He and I realized instantly that we had caught each other, and he began to disintegrate before my eyes from the top on down." A little later, Leslie Anne began "falling" out of her bed–eventually winding up on the far side of her room. Two days after the last "fall," the little girl came down to breakfast and asked if her mother had come up to check on her the night before.

Little Leslie Anne then told her mother about the lady with the pretty, long blond hair and white dress that came to see her. "She asked me to go with her...and I told her I could not go with somebody I did not know, I had to ask my Mom and she said she'd come back..., " reported Leslie.

"How did you explain *that* to the little girl?" I wondered out loud. "I think we discussed angels rather vaguely and let it go at that," Nancy replied. "But our children are brought up to accept life after death, so she was not upset."

As if the man disintegrating in her bedroom and the blond lady were not enough extra population, Nancy also noticed some "white spots on the wall" in the bedroom. She had the uncanny feeling that Ella Hauser, the woman who built their house, was still around checking up on them.

Tom Jones is a man with a practical, down-to-earth outlook, despite his experiences with the uncanny. But the situation involving his tools was too much even for him.

"I was working with Sheetrock, and I used a very heavy flat-headed hammer. I left it up on the third floor one night, but when I went up there early next morning, the hammer was gone. Finally, I found it tucked in a little crevice in the wall. Then my nails started to disappear...then my Sheetrock knife." "And where did you find them afterwards?" I asked. "Under things that I know I couldn't have put them under. It felt like somebody didn't want me to finish that attic....the job should have taken six weeks. It took me about four months, with all those interruptions."

But the Joneses were not alone in their encounters with the unknown. In August 1977, a babysitter, also named Nancy, had just put the two girls to bed up on the third floor. All of a sudden Nancy heard someone going through the drawers downstairs. "She thought maybe someone was opening and closing the drawers looking for something, and her first thought was, it's Prudence the cat doing it," Nancy Jones said. "But then she rocked the baby a little more, and underneath the rocker, there was the cat. When she came downstairs nothing had been touched." That was one babysitter lost to the Joneses. Nothing would get her to go back to "that house" again. About that time there had been a number of robberies in the area, so it was natural for Nancy Jones to think they had a prowler in the house the night she went downstairs for a drink and found a five foot, ten inches man standing in her living room, at three in the morning. "I was so scared when I saw his black belt buckle, one of the khaki shirts farmers wear, and a pair of brown work pants. Everything was too big for the guy, I could tell it was an old man. I took one look and ran upstairs. I told my husband; he said, let's wait." I seemed perplexed by that, so Tom added,"You see, he might have had a gun. I didn't. We had agreed that if the prowler came to the top of the stairs, we would defend ourselves and the children. We had a baseball bat in the closet, but hopefully since he had been observed, he would leave." Nancy described the prowler as solid. "I couldn't see *through him* like the other one....he seemed like a real, live human being standing in my living room at three o'clock in the morning, with the house locked up tight," she said.

"We went down the next morning," Tom Jones continued, "nothing had been touched. Even the dust was intact on every window sill. Doors and windows still locked. Basement door locked. There was no way a man could have gotten in or out."

By that time the Joneses felt they needed professional advice, so they got in touch with me. They had read some of my books and thought I could supply some answers to the puzzle. I agreed to have a look. While they were waiting for me, the phenomena moved into their kitchen.

"Three weeks ago I came in late one night, and I saw what appeared to be some kind of fog in ourkitchen," Nancy reported "There was a strange haze all over the top of the room. We have a Fisher stove in the kitchen but it hadn't been lit that evening."

Nancy realized that some unseen force or person was giving her the once-over, especially as they were constantly changing things around in the house, trying to make it as comfortable to their own taste as they could.

"One day I was in the kitchen, and about to put a glass on the second shelf. The next thing I knew the glass fell out of the shelf, went all the way into the back of the bottom shelf and broke three other glasses inside. In plain daylight."

"What did you do?" I asked.

"I screamed, 'Leave my glasses alone!' If you deal with this thing, it backs off...," replied Nancy.

"Is it still around...I mean, *them?*"

Nancy nodded emphatically.

"They must have known you were coming, Dr. Holzer. The last thing was this morning in the loft. Tom comes home early in the morning because he works the night shift. The door is always locked. Today I wanted to surprise him, so I *unlocked* the door, just so I could see the surprise on his face when he came in. But when he came home five minutes later, the door was locked tight. *I didn't lock that door.*"

I've met thousands of people who have problems with ghosts. Some are frightened, some laugh at it and try to ignore it, some exaggerate their problems into Amityville horror-type stories–and some come to terms with it, like the Joneses.

"I've gone from thinking it was funny to not thinking it was funny to being traumatized to total frustration and back to thinking it was funny, to learning to live with it...I've made my peace with *her.* I'd like her to leave, because it's my house. The old saying is true, you cannot put two women in one house. It's my house, it's not hers anymore," commented Nancy.

I asked how the neighbors felt about the house, the Joneses...and *them.*

"Oh, we're known as the nuts that live down the road," Nancy shrugged." Of course I'm tired of being laughed at, so I don't talk about it anymore."

"I can't deny that these things happened," Tom added calmly, "they did. I don't get excited about them. I've dealt with the trauma, it's just another assignment to me. But I ask myself, why all of a sudden so many revelations about life after death and reincarnation? Surely, our situation is far from unique. Maybe contemporary religion is out of focus with what's really happening?"

"Do you discuss it with people at work?" I inquired.

"You don't bring it up in open conversation...you find a common denominator and pretty soon you bring out from various people incidents that they can't explain."

I asked Tom how he felt about Ella, who built the house and was loathe to leave it, even in death?

He thought about my question for a moment.

"Ella and I get along fine because I can go to bed at night and not feel bothered. My feeling is, Ella you got your space, I've got mine. Just don't bother the kids, don't bother our lifestyle, we've got work to do."

The Jones know what it's like to live with ghosts *firsthand*.

Having heard and recorded the various testimonies in respect to Ella's presence, I then took some black-and-white and some color pictures of the house and the garden.

The stairs leading to the upper story somehow attracted my immediate attention. I took several black-and-white pictures of it in ordinary room light, using my Zeiss camera and fast film. It was evening.

When the pictures came back from the professional lab, I was surprised to see that Ella had indeed had the last word.

On one picture of the staircase, taken from a steady surface, a whitish figure seems to descend the stairs. In a second shot from the same roll Ella herself appears, having apparently managed to gather up enough psychic energy to do so. With her, she brought what appears to be a pet dog, maybe even two. When you look at this ghostly portrait, you cannot help but notice the grim determination of the lady of the house to have her way–even in death.

Photo 67 Psychic photo of staircase.

Date:

April 1979.

Place:

Vineland, New Jersey,
home of the Joneses.

Light conditions:

Ordinary electric room
light.

Camera:

Super Ikonta B by Zeiss.

Film:

120 black-and-white fast
film.

Exposure:

1/50 second.

Operator:

Dr. Hans Holzer.

Developing and printing:

Professional lab.

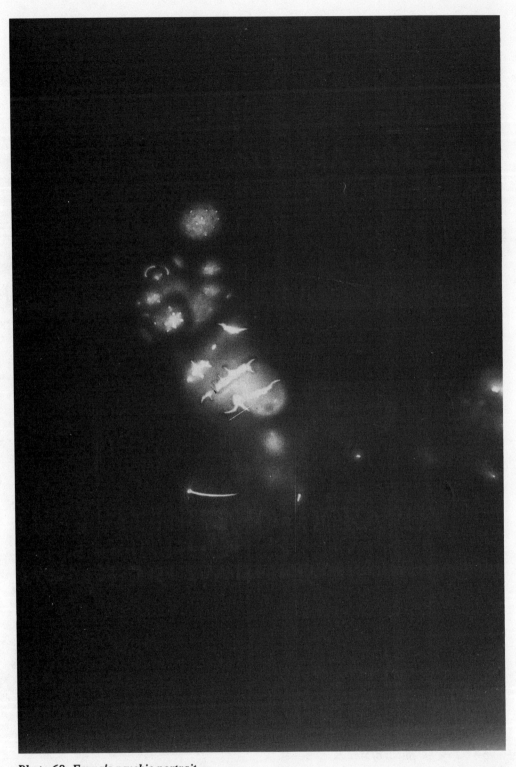

Photo 68   Emma's psychic portrait.

XXII
THE RESTLESS
GHOST OF THE
SEA CAPTAIN

When a New England salt has a grievance, he can sometimes take it to his grave. That is, if he *were* in his grave. In this case the sea captain in question never really passed away completely. He is still in what used to be his house, pushing people around and generally frightening one and all.

Spending time in this house is not easy. But I did, and somehow survived the night.

Some of the best leads regarding a good ghost story come to me as the result of my having appeared on one of many television or radio programs, usually discussing a book dealing with the subject of psychic phenomena. So it happened that one of my many appearances on the Bob Kennedy television show in Boston drew unusually heavy mail from places as far away as other New England states and even New York.

Now if there is one thing ghosts don't really care much about it is time–to them everything is suspended in a timeless dimension where the intensity of their suffering or problem remains forever constant and alive. After all, they are unable to let go of what it is that ties them to a specific location, otherwise they would not be what we so commonly (and perhaps a little callously) call ghosts. I am mentioning this as a way of explaining why, sometimes, I cannot respond as quickly as I would like to when someone among the living reports a case of a haunting that needs to be looked into. Reasons were and are now mainly lack of time but more likely lack of funds to organize a team and go after the case. Still, by and large, I do manage to show up in time and usually manage to resolve the situation.

Thus it happened that I received a letter dated August 4, 1966, sent to me via station WBZ-TV in Boston, from the owner of Cap'n Grey's Smorgasbord, an inn located in Barnstable on Cape Cod. The owner, Lennart Svensson, had seen me on the show.

"We have experienced many unusual happenings here. The building in which our restaurant and guest house is located was built in 1716 and was formerly a sea captain's residence," Svensson wrote.

I'm a sucker for sea captains haunting their old houses so I wrote back asking for details. Svensson replied a few weeks later, pleased to have aroused my interest. Both he and his wife had seen the apparition of a young woman, and their eldest son had also felt an unseen presence; guests in their rooms also mentioned unusual happenings. It appeared that when the house was first built the foundation had been meant as a fortification against Indian attacks. Rumor has it, Svensson informed me, that the late sea captain had been a slave trader and sold slaves on the premises.

Svensson and his wife, both of Swedish origin, had lived on the Cape in the early 1930s, later moved back to Sweden, to return in 1947. After a stint working in various restaurants in New York, they acquired the inn on Cape Cod.

I decided a trip to the Cape was in order. I asked Sybil Leek to accompany me as the medium. Svensson explained that the inn would close in October for the winter, but he, and perhaps other witnesses to the phenomena, could be seen even after that date, should I wish to come up then. But it was not until June 1967, the following year, that I finally contacted Svensson to set a date for our visit. Unfortunately, he had since sold the inn and, as he put it, the new owner was not as interested in the ghost as he was, so there was no way for him to arrange for our visit now.

But Svensson did not realize how stubborn I can be when I want to do something. I never gave up on this case, and decided to wait a little and then approach the new owners. Before I could do so, however, the new owner saw fit to get in touch with me instead. He referred to the correspondence between Svensson and myself, and explained that at the time I had wanted to come up, he had been in the process of redoing the inn for its opening. That having taken place several weeks ago, it would appear that "we have experienced evidence of the spirit on several occasions, and I now feel we should look into this matter as soon as possible." He invited us to come on up whenever it was convenient, preferably yesterday.

The new owner turned out to be a very personable attorney named Jack Furman of Hyannis. When I wrote we would indeed be pleased to meet him, and the ghost or ghosts as the case might be, he sent us all sorts of information regarding flights and offered to pick us up at the airport. Furman was not shy in reporting his own experiences since he had taken over the house.

"There has been on one occasion an umbrella mysteriously stuck into the stairwell in an open position. This was observed by my employee, Thaddeus B. Ozimek. On another occasion when the inn was closed in the early evening, my manager returned to find the front door bolted from *the inside* which appeared strange since no one was in the building. At another time, my chef observed that the heating plant went off at 2:30 A.M., and the serviceman, whom I called the next day, found that a fuse was removed from the fuse box. At 2:30 in the morning, obviously, no one that we know of was up and around to do this. In addition, noises during the night have been heard by occupants of the inn."

I suggested in my reply that our team, consisting of Sybil Leek, Catherine (my wife at the time), and myself, should spend the night at the inn as good ghost hunters do. I also requested that the former owner, Svensson, be present for further questioning, as well as any direct witnesses to phenomena. On the other hand, I delicately suggested that no one not concerned with the case should be present, keeping in mind some occasions where my investigations had been turned into entertainment by my hosts to amuse and astound neighbors and friends.

The date for our visit was scheduled for August 17, 1967 – a year and two weeks after the case first came to my attention. But not much of a time lag, the way it is with ghosts.

When we arrived at the inn, after a long and dusty journey by car, the sight that greeted us was well worth the trip. There, set back from a quiet country road amid tall, aged trees, sat an impeccable white colonial house, two stories high with an attic, nicely surrounded by a picket fence, and an old bronze and iron lamp at the corner. The windows all had their wooden shutters opened to the outside and the place presented such a picture of peace that it was difficult to realize we had come here to confront a disturbance. The house was empty, as we soon realized, because the new owner had not yet allowed guests to return – considering what the problems were!

Soon after we arrived at the house, Sybil Leek let go of her conscious self in order to immerse herself in the atmosphere and potential presences of the place.

"There is something in the bedroom...in the attic," Sybil said immediately as we climbed the winding stairs. "I thought just now someone was pushing my hair up from the back," she then added.

Mr. Furman had, of course, come along for the investigation. At this point we all saw a flash of light in the middle of the room. None of us was frightened by it, not even the lawyer who by now had taken the presence of the supernatural in his house in stride.

We then proceeded downstairs again, with Sybil Leek assuring us that whatever it was that perturbed her up in the attic did not seem to be present downstairs. With that we came to a locked door, a door that Mr. Furman assured us had not been opened in a long time. When we managed to get it open, it led us to the downstairs office or the room now used as such. Catherine, ever the alert artist and designer that she was, noticed that a door had been barred from the inside, almost as if someone had once been kept in that little room. Where did this particular door lead to, I asked Mr. Furman. It led to a narrow corridor and finally came out into the fireplace in the large main room.

"Someone told me if I ever dug up the fireplace," Furman intoned significantly, "I might find something."

What that something would be, was left to our imagination. Furman added that his informant had hinted at some sort of valuables, but Sybil immediately added, "bodies...you may find bodies."

She described, psychically, many people suffering in the house, and a secret way out of the house–possibly from the captain's slave trading days?

Like a doctor examining a patient, I then examined the walls both in the little room and the main room and found many hollow spots. A bookcase turned out to be a false front. Hidden passages seemed to suggest themselves. Quite obviously, Furman was not about to tear open the walls to find them. But Mrs.Leek was right: the house was honeycombed with areas not visible to the casual observer.

Sybil insisted we seat ourselves around the fireplace, and I insisted that the ghost, if any, should contact us there rather than our trying to chase the elusive phantom from room to room. "A way out of the house is very important,"Mrs. Leek said, and I couldn't help visualizing the unfortunate slaves the good (or not so good) captain had held captive in this place way back.

But when nothing much happened, we went back to the office, where I discovered that the front portion of the wall seemed to block off another room beyond it, not accounted for when measuring the outside walls. When we managed to pry it open, we found a stairwell, narrow though it was, where apparently a flight of stairs had once been. Catherine shone a flashlight up the shaft, and we found ourselves below a toilet in an upstairs bathroom! No ghost here.

We sat down again, and I invited the presence, whomever it was, to manifest. Immediately Mrs. Leek remarked she felt a young boy around the place, a 150 years ago. As she went more and more into a trance state, she mentioned the name Chet...someone who wanted to be safe from an enemy...Carson...

"Let him speak," I said.

"Carson ... 1858 ..., " Sybil replied, now almost totally entranced as I listened carefully for words coming from her in halting fashion.

"I will fight ... Charles ... the child is missing ..."

"Whom will you fight? Who took the child?" I asked in return.

"Chicopee...child is dead."

"Whose house is this?"

"Fort..."

"Whose is it?"

"Carson..."

"Are you Carson?"

"Captain Carson."

"What regiment?"

"Belvedere...cavalry...9th..."

"Where is the regiment stationed?"

There was no reply.

"Who commanded the regiment?" I insisted.

"Wainwright ... Edward Wainwright ... commander."

"How long have you been here?"

"Four years."

"Where were you born?"

"Montgomery ... Massachusetts."

"How old are you now?"

There was no reply.

"Are you married?"

"My son ... Tom ... ten ..."

"What year was he born in?"

"Forty ... seven ..."

"Your wife's name?"

"Gina..."

"What church do you go to?"

"I don't go."

"What church do you belong to?"

"She is ... of Scottish background ... Scottish kirk."

"Where is the kirk located?"

"Six miles..."

"What is the name of this village we are in now?"

"Chicopee ..."

Further questioning provided more information. We learned that "the enemy" had taken his boy, and the enemy were the Iroquois. This was his fort and he was to defend it. I then began, as I usually do, when exorcism is called for, to speak of the passage of time and the need to realize that the entity communicating through the medium was aware of the true situation in this respect. Did Captain Carson realize that time had passed since the boy had disappeared?

"Oh yes," he replied. "Four years."

"No, a hundred and seven years," I replied.

Once again I established that he was Captain Carson, and there was a river nearby and Iroquois were the enemy. Was he aware that there were "others" here besides himself.

He did not understand this. Would he want me to help him find his son since they had both passed over and should be able to find each other there?

"I need permission ... from Wainwright ..."

As I often do in such cases, I pretended to speak for Wainwright and granted him the permission. A ghost, after all, is not a rational human being but an entity existing in a delusion where only emotions count.

"Are you now ready to look for your son?"

"I am ready."

"Then I will send a messenger to help you find him," I said, "but you must call out to your son ... in a loud voice."

The need to reach out to a loved one is of cardinal importance in the release of a trapped spirit, commonly called a ghost.

"John Carson is dead ... but not dead forever," he said in a faint voice.

"You lived here in 1858, but this is 1967," I reminded him.

"You are mad!"

"No, I'm not mad. Touch your forehead ... you will see this is not the body you are accustomed to. We have lent you a body to communicate with us. But it is not yours."

Evidently touching a woman's head did jolt the entity from his beliefs. I decided to press on.

"Go from this house and join your loved ones who await you outside..."

A moment later Captain Carson had slipped away and a sleepy Leek opened her eyes.

I now turned to Furman, who had watched the proceedings with mounting fascination. Could he corroborate any of the information that had come to us through the entranced medium?

"This house was built on the foundations of an Indian fort," he confirmed, "to defend the settlers against the Indians."

"Were there any Indians here in 1858?"

"There are Indians here even now," Furman replied. "We have an Indian reservation at Mashpee, near here, and on Martha's Vineyard there is a tribal chief and quite a large Indian population."

We later learned that Chicopee Indians were indeed in this area. Also there was an Indian uprising in Massachusetts as late as the middle of the nineteenth century, giving more credence to the date, 1858, that had come through Mrs. Leek.

He also confirmed having once seen a sign in the western part of Massachusetts that read "Montgomery" – the place Captain Carson had claimed as his birthplace. Also that a Wainwright family was known to have lived in an area not far from where we were now.

However, Furman had no idea of any military personnel by that name.

"Sybil mentioned a river in connection with this house," I noted. Furman said, "And, yes, there is a river running through the house, it is still here."

Earlier Sybil had drawn a rough map of the house as it was in the past, from her psychic viewpoint, a house surrounded by a high fence. Furman pronounced the drawing amazingly accurate – especially as Leek had not set foot on the property or known about it until our actual arrival.

"My former secretary, Carole E. Howes, and her family occupied this house," Furman explained when I turned my attention to the manifestations themselves. "They operated this house as an inn twenty years ago, and often had unusual things happen here as she grew up, but it did not seem to bother them. Then the house passed into the hands of a Mrs. Nielson; then Svensson took over. But he did not speak of the phenomena until about a year and a half ago. The winter of 1965 he was shingling the roof, and he was just coming in from the roof on the second floor balcony on a cold day – he had left the window ajar and secured – when suddenly he heard the window sash come down. He turned around on the second floor platform and he saw the young girl, her hair windswept behind her. She was wearing white. He could not see anything below the waist, and he confronted her for a short period, but could not bring himself to talk – and she went away. His wife was in the kitchen sometime later, in the afternoon, when she felt the presence of someone in the room. She turned around and saw an older man dressed in black at the other end of the kitchen. She ran out of the kitchen and never went back in again.

"The accountant John Dillon's son was working in the kitchen one evening around ten. Now some of these heavy pots were hanging there on pegs from the ceiling. Young Dillon told his father two of them lifted themselves up from the ceiling, unhooked themselves from the pegs, and came down on the floor."

Did any guests staying at the inn during Svensson's ownership complain of any unusual happenings?

"There was this young couple staying at what Svensson called the honeymoon suite," Furman replied. "At 6:30 in the morning, the couple heard three knocks at the door, three loud, distinct knocks, and when they opened the door, there was no one there. This sort of thing had happened before."

Another case involved a lone diner who complained to Svensson that "someone" was pushing him from his chair at the table in the dining room onto another chair, but since he did not see another person, how could this be? Svensson hastily explained that the floor was a bit rickety and that was probably the cause.

Was the restless spirit of the captain satisfied with our coming? Did he and his son meet up in the Great Beyond? Whatever came of our visit, nothing further has been heard of any disturbances at Cap'n Grey's Inn in Barnstable.

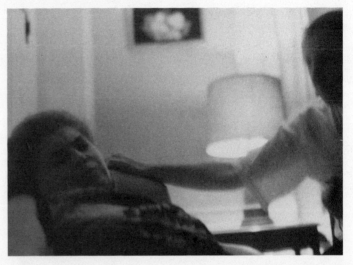

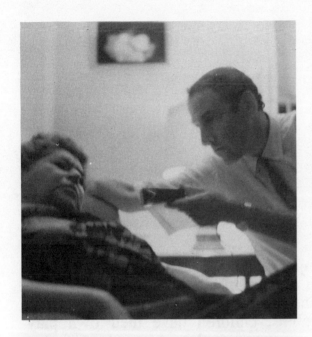

Photos 69, 70, 71 Professor Holzer interrogating medium Sybil Leek, who is already in a trance. Notice photos 70 and 71. In photo 71 the lamp becomes transparent, and Holzer's arm now appears to be behind *the lamp!*

HOW THESE PICTURES WERE OBTAINED

Date:

August 1967.

Place:

The Cap'n Grey Inn,
The haunted room,
Barnstable (Cape Cod)
Massachusetts.

Light conditions:

Nighttime, electric
room light.

Camera:

Super Ikonta B (Zeiss).

Film:

Ectacolor print film,
120.

Exposure:

1.50 second.

Operator:

Hans Holzer.

137

XXIII
THE GHOST MONKS
OF AETNA SPRINGS

If you like golf, you'll enjoy our nine-hole golf course," says the brochure put out by the Aetna Springs, California, resort. The resort boasts a really fine self-contained vacationland. People live in comfortable cabins, children have their own playground, adults can play whatever games *they* please, there are tennis, swimming, fishing, riding, dancing, horseshoe pitching, hunting, shuffleboarding, mineral bathing–the springs–and last, but certainly not least, there is that lovely golf course stretching for several miles on the other side of the only road leading up to the place. With all the facilities on one side of the road, the golf course looks like a million miles from nowhere. I don't know if it pleases the guests, but it is fine with the *ghosts*. For I did not come up 85 miles north of San Francisco to admire the scenery, of which there is plenty to admire.

As the road from Napa gradually enters the hills, you get the feeling of being in a world that really knows little of what goes on outside. The fertile Napa Valley and its colorful vineyards soon give way to a winding road and before you know it you're deep in the woods. Winding higher and higher, the road leads past scattered human habitation into the Pope Valley. Here there was a mineral spring with health properties at the far end of the golf course.

In the old days, such a well would naturaly be the center of any

138

settlement, but today the water is no longer commercially bottled. You can get as much as you want for free at the resort, though.

Incidentally there are practically no other houses or people within miles of Aetna Springs. The nearest village is a good 20 minutes' ride away over rough roads.

But we had not come up all this way for the mineral water. Bill Wyn, a young engineer from San Francisco, was driving my ex-wife Catherine, Sybil Leek and me in his fiance Lori Clerf's car. Sybil did not have the faintest idea why we were here. She honestly thought it was an excursion for the sheer joy of it, but then she knows me well and suspected an ulterior motive, which indeed was not long in coming.

My interest in this far-off spot started in 1965 when I met Dr. Andrew von Salza for the first time. He is a famous rejuvenation specialist and about as down to earth a man as you can find. Being a physician made him even more skeptical about anything smacking of the occult. It was therefoe with considerable disbelief, even disdain, that he discovered a talent he had not bargained for: he was a photographic medium with rare abilities.

The reason for our somewhat strenuous trip to Aetna Springs had its origin in another visit paid the place in 1963 by von Salza. At that time, he took two pictures with a stereo camera owned by Mr. Heibel, the manager of the resort.

As soon as the pictures were developed, von Salza and Heibel were in for a big surprise. Heibel's exposures showed the magnificent golf course and nothing more. But von Salza's pictures, taken at the same time, clearly had *two rows of monks* on them. There were perhaps eight or ten monks wearing white robes, with shaven heads, carrying lighted candles in their outstretched hands. Around them, especially around their heads, were flame-like emanations.

There was no doubt about it, these are color photographs of monks who died in flames–unless the fiery areas represent life energy. They were brightest around the upper parts of the bodies. On one of the pictures, the monks walk to the right, on the other, to the left, but in both exposures you can clearly distinguish their ascetic hollow-eyed faces–as if they had suffered terribly.

The pictures were not only fascinating, they were upsetting, even to me, and I have often been successful in psychic photography. Here we had a scientific document of the first order.

I wanted to know more about these monks, and the only way to find out was to go up to Napa County. That is why we were winding our way through the Pope Valley that warm October afternoon.

Date:

Late summer of 1963. Afternoon.

Place:

The golf course at Aetna Springs, St. Helena, California.

Light conditions:

Bright, sunny afternoon.

Camera:

Wollensack stereo camera.

Film:

Color stereo film, daytime, 160 ASA.

Exposure:

1/250 second at F/16.

Operator:

Dr. Andrew von Salza, with Mr. Heibel's camera.

Developing:

San Francisco photography shop.

Photo 72 and 72A The ghost monks.

We were still many miles away from Aetna Springs when Sybil took my hand and said:

"The place you're taking me is a place where a small group of people must have gone for sanctuary, for survival, and there is some *religious element present.*"

"What happened there?"

"They were completely wiped out."

"What sort of people were they, and who wiped them out?"

"I don't know why, but the word 'Anti-Popery' comes to me. Also a name, Hi...."

A little later, she felt the influence more strongly.

"I have a feeling of people crossing water, not native to California. A Huguenot influence?"

When we passed a sign on the road reading "Red Silver Mines," Leek remarked she had been impressed with treasures of precious metals and the trouble that comes with them.

We had now arrived at the resort. For 15 minutes we walked around it until finally we encountered a surly caretaker, who directed us to the golf course. We drove as far onto it as we could, then we left the car behind and walked out onto the lawn. It was a wide open area, yet Sybil instantly took on a harrowed look as if she felt closed in.

"Torture ... crucifixion and fire ...," she mumbled, somewhat shaken. "Why do we have to go through it?"

I insisted. There was no other way to find out if there was anything ghostly there.

"There is a French Protestant Huguenot influence here ...," she added, "but it does not seem to make sense. Religion and anti-religion. The bench over there by the trees is the center of activity ... some wiping out took place there, I should think ... crosses ... square crosses, red, blood crosses...."

"What nationality are they, these people?"

"Conquistadores..."

"Who were the victims?"

"I'm trying to get just one word fixed ... H-I ... I can't get the rest ... it has meaning to this spot ... many presences here...."

"How many?"

"Nine."

"How are they dressed?"

"Like a woman's dress on a man...skirted dress."

"Color?"

"Brown."

"Do they have anything in their hands or doing anything, any action?"

"They have a thing around their head ... like the Ku Klux Klan ... can't see their faces ... light ... fire light ... fire is very important ..."

When I asked her to look closer, she broke into tears. "No, No," she begged off, her fists clenched, tears streaming down her cheeks. I had never seen her emotionally involved that much in a haunting.

"What do you feel?" I asked softly. She was almost in trance now.

"Hate ...," she answered with a shaky voice choked with tears, "to be found here, secretly, *no escape* ... from the Popish people...no faces...."

"Did they perish in this spot?" I asked.

Almost inaudibly Sybil's voice replied:

"Yes...."

"Are the people, these nine, still here?"

"Have to be...Justice for their lives...."

"Who has hurt them?"

"Hieronymus." There was the "Hi" she had tried to bring out before.

"Who's Hieronymus?"

"The leader of the Popish people."

"What did he do to them?"

"He burned them...useless."

"Who were they?"

"They took the silver..."

I intoned some words of compassion and asked the nine ghosts to join their brothers since the ancient wrong done them no longer mattered.

"Pray for us," Sybil muttered. "Passed through the fire, crosses in hand ... their prayers...."

Sybil spoke the words of a prayer in which I joined. Her breath came heavily as if she were deeply moved. A moment later the spell broke and she came out of it. She seemed bewildered and at first had no recollection where she was.

"Must go ...," she said and headed for the car without looking back.

It was some time before we could get her to talk again, a long way from the lonely golf course gradually sinking into the October night.

Sybil was herself again and she remembered nothing of the previous hour. But for us, who had stood by her when the ghostly monks told their story, as far as they were able to, not a word was forgotten. If recollection should ever dim, I had only to look at the photographs again that had captured the agony in which these monks had been frozen on the spot of their fiery deaths.

I took a motion picture film of the area but it showed nothing unusual, and my camera, which sometimes does yield ghost pictures, was unfortunately empty when I took some exposures. I thought I had film in it but later discovered I had forgotten to load it ... or had the hand of fate stayed my efforts?

Nobody at Aetna Springs had ever heard of ghosts or monks on the spot. So the search for corroboration was started back home.

At the Hispanic Society in New York, books about California are available only for the period during which that land was Spanish, although they do have some general histories as well.

In one of these, Irving Richman's *California under Spain and Mexico,* I was referred to a passage about the relationship between native Indian populations and their Spanish conquerors that seemed to hold a clue to the puzzle.

The specific passage referred to conditions in Santo Domingo, but it was part of the overall struggle then going on between two factions among the Spanish-American clergy. The conquistadores treated the native population only slightly less cruelly than Hitler's Nazis treated subjugated people during World War II.

Their methods of torture had not yet reached such infernal effectiveness in the 16th century, but their intentions were just as evil.

We read of Indians being put to death at the whim of the colonists, of children thrown to the dogs, of rigid suppression of all opposition, both political and spiritual, to the ruling powers.

Northern California, especially the area above San Francisco, must have been the most remote part of the Spanish world imaginable, and yet outposts existed beyond the well-known missions and their sub-posts.

One of these might have occupied the site of that golf course near the springs. Thus, whatever transpired in the colonial empire of Spain would eventually have found its way, albeit belatedly, to the backwoods also, perhaps finding conditions there that could not be tolerated from the point of view of the government.

The main bone of contention at that time, the first half of the 16th century, was the treatment and status of the native Indians. Although without political voice or even the slightest power, the Indians had some friends at court. Strangely enough, the protectors of the hapless natives turned out to be the Dominican friars–the very same Dominicans who were most efficient and active in the Spanish Inqusition at home!

Whether because of this, or for political expediency, the white-robed Dominicans opposed the brown-robed Franciscans in the matter of the Indians: to the Dominicans, the Indians were fellow human beings deserving every consideration and humane treatment. To the Franciscans, they were clearly none of these, even after they had been given the sacraments of Christianity!

And to the Spanish land owners, the Indians were cheap labor, slaves that could not possibly be allowed any human rights. Thus we had, circa 1530, a condition in some ways paralleling the conditions leading up to the War Between the States in 1861.

The passage Richman's book refers to comes from Sir A. Helps' *The Spanish Conquests in America* (London 1900, volume I, page 179 et seq).

The Fathers *(Jeronimite)* asked the opinions of the official persons and also of the Franciscans and Dominicans, touching the liberty of the Indians. It was very clear beforehand what the answers would be. The official persons and the Franciscans pronounced against the Indians, and the Dominicans in their favor.

The *Jeronimite Fathers*...and Sybil had insisted on a name, so important to this haunting: Hieronymus ... Latin for Jerome!

How could any of us have known of such an obscure ecclesiastical term? It took me several days of research, and plain luck, to find it at all.

XXIV
THE PUPPET
THEATRE GHOSTS

When you live and work next door to what used to be a busy undertaker's parlor, you may be in for unwanted visitors. Sometimes the line distinguishing the quick and the dead isn't all that distinct. Some people do die and get "prepared" for the trip to the next world, but aren't quite ready for it. For one thing, nobody really convinced them there *was* a next world, and when they find themselves fully "alive" in another dimension, which turns out to be neither heaven nor hell, but the world they just left, or thought they had left, matters get to be confusing.

At any rate, the late Frank Paris, famous puppeteer, learned to live with the lost souls next door who sometimes wandered into his place accidentally.

Frank Paris was a world-famous puppeteer, who also taught his art at Columbia University. He lived at number 12 Gay Street, Greenwich Village, New York City. The house is a four-story building of the kind that was popular around 1800. It is in excellent condition and is one of the jewels of the area. Gay Street is just around the corner from bustling Sixth Avenue, and it sometimes is hard to find unless you know how to get there.

Paris turned the basement into a workshop for his puppet theatre. There, too, at various times he has given performances with his favorite puppets. The second story has been turned into a duplex apartment for himself and his assistant. It is filled with odd sculpture, antiques, paintings, and other witnesses of his vast and curious tastes. There are gargoyles, devils' masks, Javanese dancers, reflecting his fertile artistic talent.

The house remained unaltered until 1924, when a new section was added, covering a garden which used to exist in back of the house. At one time, Mayor Jimmie Walker owned this house and used it for one of his lady loves. Prior to Paris' ownership it belonged to real estate broker Mary Ellen Strunsky.

Paris, his friends, and even guests have experienced the sensation of unseen entities walking up and down the stairs at night, and on at least one occasion, a man in evening dress appeared at the door, smiling politely and then dissolving into thin air before the very eyes of reputable witnesses.

I first brought the late medium Betty Ritter to the house, and she made contact with a restless entity dating back to the prohibition era. She had no idea of the connection between Mayor Walker's "friend" and the house. Later, Ethel Johnson Meyers brought through a French diplomat who complained he had been tortured here but had held on to his "secrets." There is evidence the house did exist at the time of the Revolutionary War. Medium Shawn Robbins came with me to the house for another visit, which was televised. Again, she made contact with a tortured soul who had died violently for holding on to "something." As for the gentleman in evening clothes, no one knows who he is.

On one occasion, Paris' partner took some photographs at a time when Paris felt presences all over the workshop. It must have been even more confusing for the dear departed ones who had not quite left, to find themselves staring at the outlandish and sometimes weird decorations in the theatre.

Paris' house is not open to the public, but it is worth a try to see his workshop if you are at all interested in puppets. And if you mention that you like ghosts, quite possibly someone will open the door to you...

Photo 73 Frank Paris' psychic picture.

HOW THIS PICTURE
WAS OBTAINED

Date:

Winter 1970 or 1971.

Place:

12 Gay Street, New
York City.

Light conditions:

Indoor electric lighting.

Camera:

35mm.

Operator:

Frank Paris' partner.

XXV
A "POKER PLAYING"
GHOST IN CINCINNATI

No, this ghost did not play cards. He played with a poker, a metal rod that is used to stir up the embers in a fireplace, and caused it to fly through the air some distance from its proper place.

All this happened in a splendid private residence in Clifton, an elegant suburb of Cincinnati, in 1967.

Mr.and Mrs. John Strader, of an illustrious Cincinnati family, had apparently run into the residue of a previous owner of their house or land who wanted to be acknowledged.

But the poker was not the only proof of the ghost's continued residence. Mr. Strader, an organ buff, was playing his movie theatre organ full blast, when Mrs. Strader took his photograph.

Perhaps it was the energy from the organ music so well played by Mr. Strader that gave the house ghost enough energy (and courage) to manifest: the picture clearly shows what the naked eye did not observe.

Photo 74 John Strader's psychic photograph.

Date:

1967.

Place:

Clifton, Ohio, residence of
the Straders.

Light conditions:

Daylight.

Camera:

35mm.

Operator:

Mrs. Strader.

XXVI
MR. WATERMAN
WANTS JUSTICE

I heard of the Millbrae case from Jean Grasso, a young woman who used to live in the house before she decided she was old enough to have a place of her own and consequently moved out to a nearby town called Burlingame. Jean had a big curiosity about things she cannot explain. Such as ESP.

After Jean moved out to Burlingame, she returned home for occasional weekends to be with her mother. Her mother slept in the living-dining room area upstairs, to save her the trouble of walking up and down the stairs to the bedroom level, since she had a heart condition.

On the occasions when Jean spent a weekend at home, she would sleep in her mother's former bedroom, situated directly underneath the one fixed for her on the upper level.

One night, as Jean lay awake in bed, she heard footsteps overhead. They walked across the ceiling, "as if they had no place to go."

Thinking that her mother had breathing difficulties, she raced upstairs, but found her mother fast asleep in bed. Moreover, when questioned about the footsteps the next morning, she assured her daughter she had heard nothing.

"Were they a man's footsteps or a woman's?" I asked Jean when we discussed this incident.

"A man's," she replied without hesitation.

Once in a while when she was in the dining area upstairs, she would see something out of the corner of an eye–a flash–something or somebody moving about–and as soon as she concentrated on it, it was not there. She had chalked all that up to her imagination, of course.

"When I'm coming down the steps, in the hall, I get a chill up my spine," Jean said, "as if I didn't want to continue on. My mother gets the same feelings there, too, I recently discovered."

One night when she spent the weekend at her parents' house and was just falling asleep a little after midnight, she was awakened by the sound of distant voices. The murmur of the voices was clear enough but when she sat up to listen further, they went away. She went back to sleep, blaming her imagination for the incident. But a week later, to the day, her incipient sleep was again interrupted by the sound of a human voice. This time it was a little girl's or a woman's voice crying out, "Help...help me!"

Jean jumped up so fast she could hear her heart beat in her ears. Surely, her mother had called her. Then she remembered that her mother had gone to Santa Cruz. There was nobody in the house who could have called for help. She looked outside. It was way after midnight and the surrounding houses were all dark. But the voice she had just heard had not come from the outside. It was there, right in the haunted room with her!

I interviewed Jean's mother, Adriana Grasso, a calm pleasant woman whose skepticism in psychic matters had always been pretty strong.

"We've had this house since 1957," she explained, "but it was already five years old when we bought it. The previous owners were named Stovell and they were about to lose it when we bought it. I know nothing about them beyond that."

The very first night she went to bed in the house, something tried to prevent her from doing so. Something kept pushing her back up. On the first landing of the stairs leading down to the bedroom level, something kept her from continuing on down. She decided to fight it out. Every time after that first experience she had the same impression–that she really *shouldn't* be coming downstairs!

"I hear footsteps upstairs when I'm downstairs and I hear footsteps downstairs when I'm upstairs, and there never is anyone there causing them," she complained.

On several occasions, she awoke screaming, which brought her daughter running in anxiously. To calm her, she assured her she had had a nightmare. But it was not true. On several different occasions, she felt something grabbing her and trying to crush her bones. Something held her arms pinned down. Finally, she had to sleep with the lights on, and it seemed to help.

A big crash also made the family wonder what was wrong with their house. Adriana heard it *upstairs* and her son Allen, upstairs at the same time, thought it was *downstairs*—only to discover that it was neither here nor there!

"Many times the doorbell would ring and there was no one outside," Adriana added, "but I always assumed it was the neighborhood children, playing tricks on us."

Loud noises as if a heavy object had fallen brought her into the garage to investigate, but nothing had fallen, nothing was out of place. The garage was locked and so was the front door. Nobody had gotten in. And yet the noises continued; only three days before my arrival with Sybil Leek, Adriana awoke around one in the morning to the sound of "someone opening a can in the bathroom," a metal container. In addition, there was thumping. She thought, why is my son working on his movies at this hour of the night? She assumed the can-opening noises were motion picture film cans, of which her son had many. But he had done nothing of the sort.

Mrs. Leek and I entered the house and immediately I asked Sybil for her psychic impressions. She had not had a chance to orient herself nor did I allow her to meet the Grassos officially. Whatever she might "get" now would therefore not be colored by any rational impressions of the people she met or the house she was in.

"There is something peculiar about the lower portion of the house," Sybil began, referring to the bedroom floor. The house *was* built in a most peculiar manner. Because the lot was sloping toward a ravine, the top floor reached to street level on the front side of the house only. It was here that the house had its living room and entrance hall. On the floor below were the bedrooms, and finally, a garage and adjoining workroom. Underneath was a basement, which, led to ground level in the rear, where it touched the bottom of the ravine.

"Somebody was chased here," Sybil commented now, "two men ... an accident that should never have happened ... someone died here ... *a case of mistaken identity.*"

"Can you get more?" I urged her.

"There is a lingering feeling of a man," Sybil intoned. "He is the victim. He was not the person concerned. He was running from the water's edge to a higher part of land. He was a fugitive."

Anyone coming from the San Francisco waterfront would be coming up here to higher ground.

"Whom was he running from?" I asked.

"The law ... I feel uniforms. There is an element of supposed justice in it, but..."

"How long ago was he killed?"

"1884."

"His name?"

"Wasserman ... that's how I get it. I feel the influence of his last moments here, but not his body. He wants us to know he was Wasserman but not the Wasserman wanted by the man."

"What does he look like to you?"

"Ruddy face, peculiarly deep eyes ... he's here but not particularly cooperative."

"Does he know he is *dead*?" I asked.

"I don't think he knows that. But he notices *me*."

I asked Sybil to convey the message that we knew he was innocent.

"Two names I have to get," Sybil insisted and started to spell, "Pottrene ... P-o-t-t-r-e-n-e ... Wasserman tells me these names ... P-o-v-e-y ... Povey ... he says to find them ... these people are the men who killed him."

"How was he killed?"

"The *had* to kill him. They thought that he was someone else."

"What was the other one wanted for?"

"He doesn't know. He was unfortunate to have been here."

"What is his first name?"

"Jan .J-a-n."

Upon my prodding, Sybil elicited also the information that Jan Wasserman was a native of San Francisco, that his father's name was Johan or John, and he lived at 324 Emil Street.

I proceeded then to address the ghost in my usual manner, speaking gently of the "other side" and what awaited him there.

Sybil conveyed my wishes to the restless one and reported that he understood his situation now.

"He's no trouble," Sybil murmured. She's very sympathetic to ghosts.

With that we left the basement and went back up the stairs into the haunted bedroom, where I took some photographs; then I moved into the living room area upstairs and took some more—all in all about a dozen black-and-white photographs, including some of the garage and stairs.

Imagine my pleased reaction when I discovered a week later, when the film came back from the laboratory, that two of the photographs had psychic material on them. One, taken of the stairs leading from the bedrom floor to the top floor, shows a whitish substance like a dense fog filling the front right half of my picture. The other remarkable photograph taken of Mrs. Grasso leaning against the wall in the adjoining room shows a similar substance with mirror effect, covering the front third of the area of the picture.

There is a reflection of a head and shoulders of a figure which at first glance I took to be Mrs. Grasso's. On close inspection, however, it is quite dissimilar and shows rather a heavy head of hair whereas Mrs. Grasso's hairdo is close to the head. Mrs. Grasso wears a dark housecoat over a light dress but the image shows a woman or girl wearing a dark dress or sweater over a white blouse.

I asked Jean to report to me any changes in the house after our visit.

On November 21, 1966, I heard from her again. The footsteps were gone all right, but there was still something strange going on in the house. Could there have been *two* ghosts?

Loud crashing noises, the slamming of doors, noises similar to the thumping of trash cans when no sensible reason exists for the noises were observed not only by Jean and her mother since we were there, but also by her brother and his fiancé and even the non-believing father. No part of the house seemed immune from the disturbances.

To test things, Jean slept at her mother's house soon after we left. At 11 P.M., the thumping started. About the same time Mrs. Grasso was awakened by three knocks under her pillow. These were followed almost immediately by the sound of thumping downstairs and movements of a heavy metallic can.

Photo 75 *Jean Grasso*

**HOW THESE PICTURES
WERE OBTAINED**

Date:
October 1966, afternoon.
Place:
Millbrae, California.
Light conditions:
Daylight.
Camera:
Super Iconta B (Zeiss).
Film:
Agfa Record Isopan, 120.
Expossure:
1/50 second.
Operator:
Hans Holzer.
Developing:
United Camera, New York.

Photo 76 *Mrs. Adriana-Grasso*

Photo 76

Before I could answer Jean, I had another report from her. Things were far from quiet at the house in Millbrae. Her brother's fiancé, Ellen, was washing clothes in the washing machine. She had closed and secured the door so that the noise would not disturb her intended, who was asleep in the bedroom situated next to the laundry room.

Suddenly she distinctly heard someone trying to get into the room by force, and then she felt a "presence" with her which caused her to run upstairs in panic.

About the same time, Jean and her mother had heard a strange noise from the bathroom below the floor they were then on. Jean went downstairs and found a brush on the tile floor of the bathroom. Nobody had been downstairs at the time. The brush had fallen by itself ... into the middle of the floor.

When a picture in brother Allen's room lost its customary place on the wall, the thumbtack holding it up disappeared, and the picture itself somehow got to the other side of his bookcase. The frame is pretty heavy, and had the picture just fallen off it would have landed on the floor behind the bookcase; instead it was neatly leaning against the wall on top of it. This unnerved the young man somewhat, as he had not really accepted the possibility of the uncany up to this point, even though he had witnessed some pretty unusual things himself.

Meanwhile, Jean managed to plow through the microfilm files at the San Mateo County Library in Belmont. There was nothing of interest in the newspapers for 1884, but the files were far from complete.

However, in another newspaper of the area, the *Redwood City Gazette*, there was an entry that Jean thought worth passing on for my opinion. A Captain Watterman is mentioned in a brief piece, and the fact the townspeople are glad that his bill had died and they could be well rid of it.

The possibility that Sybil heard Wasserman when the name was actually Watterman was not to be dismissed—at least not until a Jan Wasserman could be identified from the records somewhere.

Since the year 1884 had been mentioned by the ghost, I looked up that year in H.H. Bancroft's *History of California*, an imposing record of that state's history published in 1890 in San Francisco.

In Volume VII, on pages 434 and 435, I learned that there had been great irregularities during the election of 1884 and political conditions bordered on anarchy. The man who had been first Lieutenant Governor and later Governor of the state was named R.W. Waterman!

This, of course, may only be conjecture and not correct. Perhaps she really did mean Wasserman with two "*s*'s." But my search in the San Francisco Directory (Langley's) for 1882 and 1884 did not yield any Jan Wasserman. The 1881 Langley did, however, list an Ernst Wassermann, a partner in Wassermann Brothers. He was located at 24th Street and *Potrero Avenue.*

Sybil had stated that Wasserman had been killed by a certain Pottrene and a certain Povey. Pottrene as a name does not appear anywhere. Could she have meant Potrero? The name Povey, equally unusual, does, however, appear in the 1902 Langley on page 1416.

A Francis J. Povey was a foreman at Kast & Company and lived at 1 Beideman Street. It seems rather amazing that Sybil Leek would come up with such an unusual name as Povey, even if this is not the right Povey in this case. Wasserman claimed to have lived on Emil Street. There was no such street in San Francisco. There was, however, an Emma Street, listed by Langley in 1884 (page 118).

But I was destined to hear further from the Grasso residence about an incident that began back on Christmas Eve.

Jean's sister-in-law, Ellen, was sleeping on the couch upstairs in the living room. It was around two in the morning, and she could not drop off to sleep because she had taken too much coffee. While she was lying there, wide awake, she suddenly noticed the tall, muscular figure of a man, somewhat shadowy, coming over from the top of the stairs to the Christmas tree as if to inspect the gifts placed near it. At first she thought it was Jean's brother, but as she focused on the figure, she began to realize it was nobody of flesh and blood. She noticed his face now, and that it was bearded. When it dawned on her what she was seeing, and she began to react, the stranger just vanished from the spot where he had been standing a moment before. Had he come to say goodbye and had the Christmas tree evoked a long-ago Christmas holiday of his own?

Before Ellen could tell Jean about her uncanny experience, Jean herself asked if she had heard the footsteps that kept *her* awake overhead that night. They compared the time, and it appeared that the footsteps and the apparition occurred in about the same time period.

For a few days all was quiet, as if the ghost were thinking it over. But then the pacing resumed, more furiously now, perhaps because something within him had been aroused and he was beginning to understand his position.

At this point everybody in the family heard the attention-getting noises. Mrs. Grasso decided to address the intruder and to tell him that I would correct the record of his death–that I would tell the world that he was not, after all, a bad fellow, but a case of mistaken identity.

It must have pleased the unseen visitor, for things began to quiet down again, and the house settled down to an ordinary suburban existence.

XXVII
THE GHOST OF
THE PENNSYLVANIA
BOATSMAN

When I decided to spend a quiet weekend to celebrate my birthday at the picturesque Logan Inn in New Hope, Pennsylvania, I had no idea that I was not just going to sleep in a haunted bedroom, but actually get two ghosts for the "price" of one!

The lady who communicated with my companion and myself in the darkness of the silent January night via a flickering candle in room #6, provided a heart-warming experience and one I can only hope helped the restless one get a better sense of still "belonging" to the house. Mrs. Gwen Davis the proprietor, assured me that the ghost is the mother of a former owner, who simply liked the place so much she never left.

Mrs. Davis pointed me toward the Black Bass Inn in nearby Lumberville, an 18th-century pub and now hotel right on the Delaware Canal. The place is filled with English antiques of the period and portraits of Kings Charles I, II and James II, proving that this was indeed a Loyalist stronghold at one time.

I went around the place with my camera, taking any number of photographs with fast color film in existing light. The story here concerned the ghost of a young man who made his living as a canal boatsman. Today, the canal is merely a curiosity for tourists, but in

159

Date:

January 26, 1992. Day time.

Place:

Basement of the Black Bass Inn, Lumberville, Pennsylvania.

Light conditions:

Available daylight.

Camera:

Super Ikonta B (Zeiss).

Film:

Fast color print film.

Exposure:

1/50 second.

Operator:

Rosemarie Khalil.

Developing:

Adorama lab.

Photo 77 Dr. Hans Holzer and the ghost of "Hans."

the 19th century it was an active waterway for trade, bringing goods on barges down river. The canal, which winds around New Hope and some of the nearby towns gives the area a charm all its own.

In the stone basement of the Black Bass, where the apparition had been seen by a number of people over the years, according to the current owner, Herbie Ward, I took some pictures and then asked my companion to take one of me. Picture my surprise when there appeared a white shape in the picture which cannot be reasonably explained as anything but the boatsman putting in a kind of appearance for me. The boatsman died in a violent argument with another boatsman. By the way, the name of the boatsman was Hans. Maybe he felt the two Hanses ought to get in touch?

XXVIII
THE PARISH
HOUSE GHOSTS

R on and Nancy Stallings head the Maryland Committee for Psychical Research, a body of researchers I helped create some years ago. The Stallings are dedicated, scientifically oriented people. When I first met this couple, they lived with their children in a haunted house near Baltimore which I investigated and we eventually put down as a solved case.

Since then, the Stallings have taken their camera to many haunted places and come up with positive results of photographs taken under test conditions. Nancy is undoubtedly the catalyst as she is a strong medium.

Three pictures taken by Ron and Nancy at a haunted parish house in Baltimore County, are presented here for the first time in print.

Photo 78 shows Nancy, the dark woman on the right. There appear to be three figures on the doorway, one of which is indeed very clear. When the photo was taken, there wasn't anyone in that doorway.

Photo 79 shows three people standing in an empty doorway–it appeared empty when Ron took this picture!

Photo 80 shows Nancy standing on the right, being hugged by

what she described as a little girl, and two standing figures again in the same doorway. Nancy reported that they recorded a child's voice at the same time, calling out for "Mommy" and literally following the investigators around as they made their way about the premises of the old parish house.

Photo 78 Parish House in Baltimore County. Photo taken by Ron and Nancy Stallings, January 1979. Three figures, two in doorway and one next to Nancy, werre noit there when picture was taken. Nancy is the figure on the right.

Date:

January 1979.

Place:

Parish House, Baltimore County.

Light conditions:

Natural daylight.

Camera:

35mm.

Film:

Fast black-and-white.

Exposure:

1/50 second.

Operators:

Ron and Nancy Stallings.

Developing:

Local Maryland lab.

Photo 79

Photo 80 Parish House in Baltimore County. Photo taken by Ron and Nancy Stallings, January, 1979. Two figures in doorway were not there when picture was taken. Also, notice the little girl that is hugging Nancy around the waist. On Ron and Nancy's tape recording there is a child's voice that seems to be following Nancy throughout the house saying, "Mommy." Nancy is the figure to the right of the picture. The figure next to her was not there either..

Photo 80

XXIX
THE CONFUSED
GHOST OF THE
TRAILER PARK

I met Rita Atlanta when she worked in a Frankfurt, Germany, nightclub. That is when I first heard about her unsought ability to communicate with spirits.

Later that year, after my return to New York, I received what appeared to be an urgent communication from her.

Rita's initial letter merely requested that I help her get rid of her ghost. Such requests are not unusual, but this one was—and I am not referring to the lady's occupation—exotic dancing in sundry nightclubs around the more or less civilized world.

What made her case unusual was the fact that "her" ghost appeared in a 30-year-old trailer near Boston.

"When I told my husband that we had a ghost," she wrote, "he laughed and said, 'Why should a respectable ghost move into a trailer? We have hardly room in it ourselves with three kids.'"

It seemed the whole business had started during the summer when the specter made its first sudden appearance. Although her husband could not see what she saw, Miss Atlanta's pet skunk evidently didn't like it and moved into another room. Three months

165

later, her husband passed away and Miss Atlanta was kept busy hopping the Atlantic (hence her stage name) in quest of nightclub work.

Ever since her first encounter with the figure of a man in her Massachusetts trailer, the dancer had kept the lights burning all night long. As someone once put it, "I don't believe in ghosts, but I'm scared of them."

Despite the lights, Miss Atlanta always felt a presence at the same time that her initial experience had taken place–between three and three-thirty in the morning. It would awaken her with such a regularity that at last she decided to seek help.

In September of the previous year, she and her family had moved into a brand-new trailer in Peabody, Massachusetts. After her encounter with the ghost Rita made some inquiries about the nice grassy spot where she had chosen to park the trailer. Nothing had ever stood on the spot before. No ghost stories. Nothing. Just one little thing.

One of the neighbors in the trailer camp, which is at the outskirts of greater Boston, came to see her one evening. By this time Rita's heart was already filled with fear, fear of the unknown that had suddenly come into her life here. She freely confided in her neighbor, a girl by the name of Birdie Gleason.

To her amazement, the neighbor nodded with understanding. She, too, had felt "something," an unseen presence in her house trailer next to Rita Atlanta's.

"Sometimes I feel someone is touching me," she added.

When I interviewed Rita, I asked her to describe exactly what she saw.

"I saw a big man, almost seven foot tall, about 350 pounds, and he wore a long coat and a big hat," she reported.

But the ghost didn't just stand there glaring at her. Sometimes he made himself comfortable on her kitchen counter, with his ghostly legs dangling down from it. He was as solid as a man of flesh and blood, except that she could not see his face clearly since it was in the darkness of early morning.

Later, when I visited the house trailer with my highly sensitive camera, I took some pictures in the areas indicated by Miss Atlanta: the bedroom, the door to it, and the kitchen counter. In all three areas, strange phenomena manifested on my film. Some mirrorlike transparencies developed in normally opaque areas, which could not and cannot be explained.

166

When it happened the first time, she raced for the light and turned the switch, her heart beating wildly. The yellowish light of the electric lamp bathed the bedroom in a nighmarish twilight. But the spook had vanished. There was no possible way a real intruder could have come and gone so fast. No way out, no way in. Because this was during the time Boston was being terrorized by the infamous Boston Strangler, Rita had taken special care to double-lock the doors and secure all the windows. Nobody could have entered the trailer without making a great deal of noise. I have examined the locks and the windows–not even Houdini could have done it.

The ghost, having once established himself in Rita's bedroom, returned for additional visits–always in the early morning hours. Sometimes he appeared three times a week, sometimes even more often.

"He was staring in my direction all the time," Rita said with a slight Viennese accent, and one could see that the terror had never really left her eyes. Even three thousand miles away, the spectral stranger had a hold on the woman.

Was he perhaps looking for something? No, he didn't seem to be. In the kitchen, he either stood by the table or sat down on the counter. Ghosts don't need food–so why the kitchen?

"Did he ever take his hat off?" I wondered.

"No, never," she said and smiled. Imagine a ghost doffing his hat to the lady of the trailer!

What was particularly horrifying was the noiselessness of the apparition. She never heard any footfalls or rustling of his clothes as he silently passed by. There was no clearing of the throat as if he wanted to speak. Nothing. Just silent stares. When the visitations grew more frequent, Rita decided to leave the lights on all night. After that, she did not *see* him any more. But he was still there, at the usual hour, standing behind the bed, staring at her. She knew he was. She could almost feel the sting of his gaze.

One night she decided she had been paying huge light bills long enough. She hopped out of bed, turned the light switch to the off position and, as the room was plunged back into semidarkness, she lay down in bed again. Within a few minutes her eyes had gotten accustomed to the dark. Her senses were on the alert, for she was not at all sure what she might see. Finally, she forced herself to turn her head in the direction of the door. Was her mind playing tricks on her? There, in the doorway, stood the ghost. As big and brooding as ever.

With a scream, she dove under the covers. When she came up, eternities later, the shadow was gone from the door.

The next evening, the lights were burning again in the trailer, and every night thereafter, until it was time for her to fly to Germany for her season's nightclub work. Then she closed up the trailer, sent her children to stay with friends, and left with the faint hope that on her return in the winter, the trailer might be free of its ghost. But she wasn't at all certain.

It was obvious to me that this exotic dancer was a medium, as only the psychic can "see" apparitions.

HOW THESE PICTURES WERE OBTAINED

Date:

November 1966.

Place:

Trailer camp at Peabody, near Boston, Massachusetts.

Light conditions:

Late afternoon light.

Camera:

Super Ikonta B (Zeiss).

Film:

Agfa Record Isopan, 120.

Exposure:

Firm surface, 2 seconds.

Operator:

Hans Holzer.

Developing and printing:

United Camera, New York City.

Photo 81 Rita Atlanta.

XXX
ETERNAL REVENGE
AT AMITYVILLE

Many people are familiar with the DeFeo murders which took place in the now infamous house on Ocean Avenue in Amityville, Long Island. My lengthy investigation has born out what was quite obvious when we came to the house with our trance medium, the late Ethel Johnson Meyers: the haunting here was not a traditional "ghost story" and related to the multiple murders–though they might indeed have been. The haunting focused on a single, angry entity whose burial ground the house stood on, and nothing more.

It was the Indian chief whose tomb had been violated around the turn of the century, when the rains had exposed his skeleton and a youngster broke off the skull.

All the disturbances in that house since–and into the future, one presumes–stem from this fact.

The terrible events in the house have perhaps overshadowed the earlier misdeed, but it is my conviction that the DeFeo crimes were due to possession of young Ronald DeFeo by the avenging Indian chief, and not by his own volition at all. When I interviewed the young man in his cell at Dannemora Maximum Security Prison, the Indian did not allow me to put the young man into hypnotic trance so he could retrace his steps on the night of the murders.

169

But here are the facts of that night.

On the night of Friday November 13, 1974, six members of the DeFeo family were brutally murdered in their beds—one of the most horrifying and bizarre mass murders of recent memory.

The lone survivor of the crime, Ronald DeFeo, Jr., who had initially notified police, was soon after arrested and formally charged with the slayings. But there are aspects to the case that have never been satisfactorily resolved.

When Ronald got up in the middle of the night, took his gun, and murdered his entire family, that wasn't him who did it, but something...someone...who got inside his body and took over. "I just couldn't stop," said DeFeo.

Was DeFeo a suitable vehicle for spirit possession? The facts of my investigation strongly suggest it. DeFeo himself does not believe in anything supernatural. He does not understand what got into him. Did he massacre his family in cold blood, or under the influence of a power from beyond this dimension?

From the outset there were strange aspects to the case: nobody seems to have heard the shots which killed six people...how was it that none of the victims resisted or ran out of the murderer's way? Did they in fact not hear the shots either?

At DeFeo's trial, two eminent psychiatrists differed sharply about the state of the murderer's sanity: Dr. Schwartz considered DeFeo psychotic at the time of the murder, while Dr. Zolan held him fully responsible for what he did. Rumors to the effect that DeFeo had first drugged his family's food (which would have explained their seeming apathy) proved groundless. The mystery remained even though DeFeo's sentence was clear: 25 years to life on each of the six counts of murder in the second degree, served consecutively—as if that mattered. Over and over DeFeo repeated the same story: yes, he had killed his family, and felt no remorse over it....but no, he didn't know why. Something...someone had gotten inside his person and forced him to shoot....going from bedroom to bedroom at 3 A.M. and exterminating the same parents, brothers and sisters he had lovingly embraced at a birthday party in the house a scant two months before the crime....whatever had gotten into DeFeo surely knew no mercy.

On January 15, 1977 I brought reputable trance medium Ethel Johnson Meyers to the house on Ocean Avenue, along with a psychic photographer to investigate what was shaping up as a case of suspected possession.

Although Meyers hadn't the slightest notion where she was or why I had brought her there, she immediately stated, "Whoever lives here is going to be the victim of all the anger...the blind fierceness....this is Indian burial ground, sacred to them." As she was gradually slipping into trance, I asked why the Indian spirits were so angry.

"A white person got to digging around and dug up a skeleton..." She described a long-jawed Indian whose influence she felt in the house. "People get to fighting with each other and they don't know why. They're driven to it because they are taken over by him." According to Meyers, the long-ago misdeed of a white settler is still being avenged, every white man on the spot is an enemy, and when a catalyst moves there, he becomes a perfect vehicle for possession...like Ronald DeFeo.

"I see a dark young man wandering around at night....like in a trance...goes beserk....a whole family is involved...," the medium said. She had tuned right into the terrible past of the house.

When the pictures taken by the psychic photographer were developed on the spot, some of them showed strange haloes exactly where the bullets had struck....my camera jammed even though it had been working perfectly just before and was fine again the minute we left the house on Ocean Avenue–a house totally empty of life as we know it and yet filled with the shades of those who have passed on yet linger for they know not where to go.

HOW THESE PICTURES WERE OBTAINED

Date:

January 13, 1977

Place:

112 Ocean Avenue, Amityville, Long Island.

Light conditions:

Afternoon daylight

Camera:

Land instantaneous camera.

Film:

Fast

Operator:

Gerri Warner.

Photo 82

Photo 83:

The two photographs, developed on the spott, show clearly how the possessing entity envelops the medium, Ethel Johnson Myers, as she is being interrogated by me in one of the murder rooms.

XXXI
MR. WHALEY
WANTS HIS DAY IN
COURT

I have often referred to the Whaley House in Old Town, San Diego, California, as "America's most haunted house," because it is one of the few very active ghost houses known to me where phenomena keep occurring and people keep having experiences. Perhaps this is due to the fact that, despite several visits by me, one with the late Sybil Leek, we never really attempted to lay the ghosts to rest in the way I have done successfully so many times elsewhere.

The Whaley House was originally built in 1857 as a two-story mansion by Thomas Whaley, a San Diego pioneer. It stands at the corner of San Diego Avenue and Harney Street and is now being kept as a museum under the guidance of June Reading; it can be visited during ordinary daylight hours. As a matter of fact, thousands of people visit it every year—not because it is haunted, but because it is an outstanding example of early American architecture. Since I published the amazing accounts of the hauntings at the Whaley House in my book *Ghosts of the Golden West,* even more visitors have come, and the added enticement of perhaps meeting up with a ghost has added to the attractions of the old mansion.

There are two stories connected by a staircase. Downstairs there is a parlor, a music room, a library, and in the annex, to the left of the entrance, there used to be the County Courthouse. At least one of the hauntings is connected with the courtroom. Upstairs there are four bedrooms, tastefully furnished in the period during which the Whaley House was at its zenith—between 1860 and 1890. The house was restored by a group of history-minded citizens in 1956. If it were not for them, there would now not be any Whaley House.

Photos 84 and 85 Ghostly photos taken at Whaley House.

HOW THESE PICTURES
WERE OBTAINED

Date:

Late 1991.

Place:

The Whaley House, San
Diego

Light conditions:

Daylight.

Camera:

35mm modern Camera.

Operator:

Doreen Turner

173

Numerous witnesses, both visitors to the house and those serving as part-time guides or volunteers, have seen ghosts here. These include the figure of a woman in the courtroom, sounds of footsteps in various parts of the house, windows opening by themselves in the upper part of the house despite the fact that strong bolts had been installed and thus they could only be opened by someone on the inside; the figure of a man in a frock coat and pantaloons standing at the top of the stairs, organ music being played in the courtroom where there is in fact an organ although at the time no one was near it and the cover closed; even a ghost dog has been seen scurrying down the hall toward the dining room. There is a black rocking chair upstairs that moves of its own volition at times, as if someone were sitting in it. A woman dressed in a green plaid gingham dress has been seen seated in one of the bedrooms upstairs. Smells include perfume and the smell of cigars. There is also a child ghost present, which has been observed by a number of people working in the house, and a baby has been heard crying. Strange lights, cool breezes, and cold spots have added to the general atmosphere of haunting permeating the entire house. It is probably one of the most actively haunted mansions in the world today.

Despite my thorough investigation with the help of Sybil Leek, arranged for by television personality Regis Philbin, some of the apparitions have remained, and reports of continuing disturbances are still coming in to me. As far as I could ascertain through the trance session with Leek, the ghosts include the builder of the house, Thomas Whaley, who had a just grievance against the city of San Diego which probably has kept him tied to the house. He had put money into certain alterations so that he could sell the house to the county to be used as a courthouse. However, his contract was never executed and he was left "holding the bag." Sybil also pinpointed a child ghost correctly, age 12, by the name of Annabelle, and named the lady ghost upstairs correctly as Anna Lannay, Thomas Waley's wife.

Photographic evidence, pictures taken mainly by Doreen Turner, one of the volunteer guides, shows quite plainly that Whaley's grievances against the city government of San Diego, have not yet been satisfied–at least not in his own, surviving mind.

It is wise to ask for a guided tour or at the very least check in with Mrs. Reading to be sure that the ghostly spots are properly pointed out. Since there are so many of them, you can hardly avoid at least one of the several hauntings at the Whaley House.

AFTERWORD

The word *science* means a state of knowing, from the Latin word *scire,* to know. It does not mean, as so many modern practitioners think, the only *proper* way to knowledge. There are other paths, just as effective and sometimes more accurate than the scientific road. You cannot supply concrete proof of mystic identification with other beings as we understand the term, but, to the experimenter, the experience itself is infinitely more accurate and direct than any scientific attempt to interpret it for him or her. Still, insofar as is possible, I am committed to the scientific approach to psychic phenomena: I will always present factual information before drawing any personal conclusions about it. Scientists in most fields disagree in their interpretation of fact, to the advantage of progress, I think, but they don't or should not disagree as to *what* these facts are.

This is where parapsychology is a difficult field, for it cannot stand on the accumulated evidence of repeatable laboratory experiment *alone*, if at all. Neither, for that matter, can oceanography or the study of volcanoes and earthquakes. They depend on qualified observation and evaluation *as well,* and it is this kind of parapsychology that I am speaking of.

There is no doubt in my mind that qualified observation is as scientific as re-creation under artificial conditions, if not more so. This is particularly true in this field where emotional factors are at the bottom of the phenomena, and where environmental influences are also significant. A psychic person fully relaxed in my living room will perform much better after some low-pressure chatting than a medium placed in a sterile cubicle in a laboratory, with the cold, uncommitted eyes of the researcher demanding results then and there. I am a researcher and I am not uncommitted. I have had significant evidence that psychic phenomena exist; my job now is to study them *further* and to learn more about them. The subject feels this and performs accordingly.

The use of subjective material, no matter how carefully screened and how well documented, still requires a basis of acceptance that the people involved—researcher and subject–are not fraudulently involved in reporting the results. Not very likely, I admit, but then some scientists, disturbed by the implications of a survival view in science, will go to great extremes to discredit that which they cannot swallow even if it is true.

I have found the camera a faithful servant, demanding neither emotional attachment nor loyalty on my part. The lens, often more sensitive than the human eye, will perform if its mechanical components are intact, and it does not manufacture anything of its own volition. Cameras and film are objective proof that what they deliver is true, provided the mechanical components are in proper shape.

Dr. Jule Eisenbud and Ted Serios have shown that men's thoughts can be put down on sensitive film at will, in what are close to controlled laboratory experiments. My own work leads the way into spontaneous field work along the same lines, while at the same time it pierces the barriers of time and space as we know them. The implications of such photography, when one realizes that fraud is impossible, are that man possesses something more than a flesh-and-blood machine called the body. It follows, therefore, that there must be some other place or state of existence where that part of man continues his being.

At the same time, I have pointed out–I am not the first one to do so, I am sure–that man's personality or soul, if you prefer, is also, in its strictest sense, an electromagnetic energy field, and as such is capable of registering on certain instruments, some already in existence, some as yet to be built. Photographic film and paper are among the tools by which man can prove his non-physical component.

It is perhaps a pity that we find it so difficult to supply the funds to establish, equip and staff an institute where psychic research is the only subject studied, where no theory is considered too far off the mark to be worthy of examination, and where scientists of every conceivable kind, persuasion and background can work hand in hand toward the greatest of all remaining "last frontiers"–inner space, man himself!

About the Author

Prof. Hans Holzer, Ph.D., is the author of over a hundred books dealing primarily with parapsychology, psychic phenomena, historical puzzles and mysteries, and has been a television writer/host/producer of reality programs, including the NBC series "In Search of..." and half a dozen special documentary programs for RKO General, Metromedia, CBS and PBS.

Prof. Holzer studied at Vienna University and Columbia University. He holds a Ph.D. from the London College of Applied Science, and lectures widely. He is listed in *Who's Who in America* and holds membership in a number of scientific societies.